Ed W

# Geordie Plays
# Vol 1

Tyne Bridge Publishing

Published by:
City of Newcastle Upon Tyne
Newcastle Libraries
Tyne Bridge Publishing, 2021

# Contents

# INTRODUCTION

The infamous film director Werner Herzog once made a film about a man who dragged a steamboat over a mountain in which he actually made the cast and crew do just that. Everyone told him he was mad yet he pressed on. Chaos ensued.

Even he wouldn't have attempted to put a play about rowing on stage. For a start there's no water.

When Ed first told me about his plan to write a play about the forgotten Geordie sculler Harry Clasper, I promptly retired from play-writing and decided to write a 90,000-word crime novel. It seemed the easier option.

Inevitably, like Mr Herzog, he pressed on, as men of vision do. But in Ed's case he succeeded. A year or so later I sat in a packed audience watching the outstanding *Hadaway Harry*, jaws dropping all around me, as the legendary rower was brought to life. Deserved standing ovations abounded at every performance.

By now Ed had a taste for chronicling the lives of Geordie heroes on stage and for his next trick he turned to the life and tunes of the Victorian music hall star, Joe Wilson. 'Nobody will come,' I said. I was wrong again. The queue for tickets went round the block. Twice.

For his hat-trick he turned to a more recent hero, Glenn McCrory, the former world champion boxer, and the bittersweet story of Glenn and his terminally-ill brother David. Having put rowing on stage, boxing held no fears at all and *Carrying David* was another triumph, juxtaposing perfectly the thrills of being at ringside with the moving story of David's too-brief life.

I'm sure there will be many more stories to come as Ed unearths more forgotten or unknown tales from Tyneside's history. Only one problem remains: who's going to write the play about the vastly underestimated Geordie legend Ed Waugh?

**TREVOR WOOD**

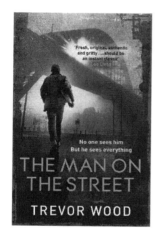

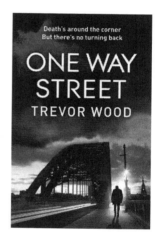

WINNER OF THE 2020 JOHN CREASEY (NEW BLOOD) DAGGER AWARD

OUT NOW!

# DIRECTOR'S NOTES.

When Ed asked me to direct the first of his 'North East' history plays, we both took a step into the unknown. On paper, *'Hadaway Harry'* appeared unworkable, yet what followed was something we'd both be proud of for the rest of our lives.

*Hadaway Harry* was theatre at its simplest, yet most challenging. Simplest, because the set was a lectern, a trunk and a projector screen, with skilled use of lights, sound and images to set the scene. Challenging, because one actor had to bring to life Harry Clasper, play all the other characters using glove puppets AND win the world rowing championship in real time sitting on a wooden chest! Cue Jamie Brown, a superb actor from Gateshead and glove puppet maestro! A theatrical sporting tour de force had been established, with standing ovations at Newcastle Theatre Royal and a 'get-out' that took only 15 minutes! Theatre at its most basic yet exhilarating. It was a rowaway success!

*The Great Joe Wilson*, another successful premiere, was a different challenge. Pure music hall, full of great songs and music, requiring a cast of talented actor/musicians, Joe Wilson had to be both moving and entertaining. Though the style was music hall, it had to be real enough to tell the great man's story. Although the show's timeframe would confound even the creators of Dr Who, it was, thanks to everyone involved, a singalong success!

*Carrying David*, another one man show, is based on Glenn McCrory's autobiography and discussions with the great boxer himself. The play seemed more conversational than *Hadaway Harry*, so I set most of the action in a bar, where the character of Glenn is explaining his life to a group of friends, i.e. you, the audience. Hence the set was a bottle of whisky, a glass, a chair and a table, and a projector screen to illustrate all the characters he talks about. It was, however, the most technical production to date, as there were over 400 sound cues alone. There was only one actor who had the talent, versatility, physical presence and comedy skills to play Glenn McCrory. Unfortunately, I wasn't available, so we cast Micky Cochrane, who had played the lead in Joe Wilson. Micky was sensational, standing ovations every night and reviews to die for. A belting success!

Ed's writing is brave, honest and funny. The key to great theatre is finding actors who are the same and I have been honoured to work with some of the North East's finest. So, keep it simple, enable the actors to work their magic, and have a great production team - my thanks to Richard and Sophie.

What have I learnt? If the show is a success, the director never gets a mention. I hope to remain incognito for many years to come.

**RUSSELL FLOYD**

# FOREWORD

It's been a privilege to see these three plays professionally performed in some of the region's top theatres. To have them preserved for posterity in a printed volume is an incredible thrill and honour; a wonderful bonus.

Words only come alive when the director, the actors...
Hadaway Harry (2015): Jamie Brown (North East tour, London and Newcastle Theatre Royal); and featuring Wayne Miller (London and Newcastle Theatre Royal, 2017).

The Great Joe Wilson (2018 North East tour): Micky Cochrane, Jamie Brown, Sarah Boulter and Jordan Miller.

Carrying David (2019): Micky Cochrane (North East and Northern Ireland tours).

...and the musical and technical teams all add their considerable talent and skills.

But for the coronavirus lockdown, Carrying David would have been the fastest-ever transfer to Newcastle Theatre Royal (scheduled for April 2020).

The fantastic research of David Clasper, Dave Harker and Glenn McCrory as well as Pete Scott's and Alex Glasgow's tremendous tunes to Joe Wilson's lyrics (and Jordan Miller's arrangements) were all integral to these projects.

Harry Clasper was a Durham miner (involved in the 1831 strike against the slavish "bond") before he became a world champion rower and coach, inventing the sport of rowing we know today with his revolutionary boat designs and skiff building.

An estimated 130,000 people stood in line to pay their respects to Harry when he died in 1870. How can someone so popular be almost forgotten only 150 years later? Sadly, history is taught in school from the perspective of kings and queens, not the working class.

Joe and Glenn were blatantly ripped off by "the money men". What makes their stories so compelling is their insuppressible determination to overcome the heavy odds stacked against them. Other people have these natural gifts but they just aren't prepared to take it to the limit like Joe (nicknamed The Bard of Tyneside) who has left us a legacy of wonderful songs and poems and Glenn, inspired by his terminally ill brother David, to become the IBF cruiserweight champion of the world.

Most of the characters in these plays speak with a Geordie accent. Writing phonetic sounds is difficult as there is no definitive spelling.

I hope the teamwork that went into celebrating these Geordie heroes on stage will keep Harry, Joe and Glenn's incredible achievements in the spotlight. Their remarkable accomplishments are an integral part of our proud working class history here in the North East of England. It's our responsibility to pass on their stories to future generations.

Thanks for buying this book. There are many more Geordie heroes and heroines out there. Hopefully see you at the next show!

Ed Waugh
June 2021

Ed Waugh

# HADAWAY HARRY

# ACT ONE

Hadaway Harry can be performed as one-man play or as a two-hander instead of using puppets.

*There is a means of showing visuals throughout the show (either a large TV within the lectern or a large projector screen). The visuals are discretionary but should be used to set the scene.*

*There is a large wooden trunk for props and for the actor to sit on.*

*This is the one-hander version of the show whereby the actor at times stands behind the lectern to voice (four) puppets, which he controls. He's also the narrator and Harry.*

*We hear the sound of 19th century heavy industry and a crowd cheering, shouting "Hadaway Harry, hadaway lads".*

*The sound fades and the narrator (in modern clothes - trousers with a vest underneath, and boots) carrying a shoulder bag, enters. He's casually singing, not eyeing the audience. He looks in the chest to take out Harry's clothes (trousers, boots and a white collarless shirt) and leaves them on top.*

**NARRATOR:** (*sings*) Aa went to Blaydon Races, 'twas on the ninth of Joon, Eiteen hundred an' sixty-two, on a summer's efternoon. Aa tyuk the 'bus frae Balmbra's, an' she wis heavy laden, away we went 'lang Collin'wood Street, that's on the road to Blaydon

*He stops and looks at the audience, smiling.*

**NARRATOR:** (*to audience*) Ahhhh, some of you were about to sing the chorus, weren't you? (*beat*) Don't worry, you'll get a chance later.

*He stands behind lectern.*

**NARRATOR:** 1862. Victorian England.

*Visual of heavy industry.*

**NARRATOR:** The Industrial Revolution, a time that changed the world - when a new and inventive capitalist class cast aside the dead hand of the landed aristocracy.

A time of great riches - and even greater poverty.

A time when villages grew rapidly into small towns, and towns into cities, as people came in from rural areas to work in large-scale industry.

A time that gave rise of the mighty industrial working class.

*He moves front stage and starts to change into Harry Clasper: Takes T-Shirt off to reveal vest.*

**NARRATOR:** A tough time, a time when playing cards and arm wrestling would often end up in fights — and that was in temperance halls.

A time when a distant relative was someone who lived in Sunderland.

A time when the best-looking lass in the Quayside was called Cushy Butterfield.

A time when...

*He holds up a Newcastle United strip.*

**NARRATOR**: ...this was but twinkle in Mike Ashley's eye.

*Visual of Newcastle Utd. Circa 1892.*

**NARRATOR**: Newcastle United didn't come into being until 1892, when football was taken up by the working class.

From 1830, it was rowing, or "aquatics", as the Victorians called it, that really fired the passion.

Now, I need to explain here...

*Visual of a sculler.*

**NARRATOR**: Rowers technically use one oar whereas scullers use two...

The oars themselves are often referred to as sculls...and the boat itself is referred to as a scull - clear as mud, eh?

Have we any rowers in tonight?

Welcome! *(beat)* Did you park your sculls outside?

*He sings softly, sitting on the chest and tying his boots as he completes his change into Harry.*

**NARRATOR**: *(sings)* An' aw got two black eyes an' a broken nose gannin' te Blaydon Races.

*A solemn Blaydon Races tune plays.*

**HARRY:** Listen.

*June 5, 1862 - Balmbra's Music Hall, Newcastle.*

**HARRY:** *The Blaydon Races*, a song written to celebrate me, Harry Clasper - a world champion rower - and my prize racing achievements.

*Visual of Geordie Ridley.*

**HARRY:** Now, divent get iz wrong, I'm obviously proud Geordie Ridley wrote it for iz, like - but between you and me, I can't see it being very popular.

Prize races...initially, they were ad hoc and sponsors put up stake money; your aristocrats, local businessmen and surprise, surprise, MPs - where's there's money you'd always find a politician...I doubt that's the same today, though.

Y'see, in my day pubs and gambling were a big part of life, and many sponsors of the oarsmen were involved with the drinks trade - importers, music hall owners...pub landlords.

So you can understand why aquatics was popular - not just with the rowers...I mean, men liked a bet.

*He's behind lectern and Geordie Woman puppet appears.*

**GEORDIE WOMAN:** Eeeeeeeee...these working men'll gamble on anything. Eeeeeeeee...I can't see the attraction of grown men cock fighting.

**HARRY:** I'm talking about rowing, man, Beatrice, man.

**GEORDIE WOMAN:** Eeeeeeeeee.

*Beatrice disappears, then quickly reappears.*

**GEORDIE WOMAN:** Eeeeeeeeee.

**HARRY:** From 1800 to 1830 rowing clubs rapidly developed throughout England - all the major rivers had them. These were mostly amateur...gentlemen's social clubs for fine dining and leisure.

**POSH GEORDIE MAN:** Well, you see, the high fees kept the riff-raff oot.

**HARRY:** But in the 1830s city regattas were established, to great public excitement. Giving a sense of local identity.

*19th Century Regatta visual.*

**HARRY:** In 1834 the Durham and Tyne Regattas were founded.

**POSH GEORDIE MAN:** The Corporation of Newcastle would like to see aal local crews tek part.

**HARRY:** Both banks of the Tyne were crowded with spectators. On the water there were no rules - and no order.

**POSH GEORDIE MAN:** Boats of aal shapes and sizes followed the racing sculls.

*Boathorn sounds.*

**HARRY:** You'd have to dodge the keels, wherries and barges and the water-churning steam boats, which meant you were rowing against their wake and, if you avoided the wash from a tug - wey, you might crash into a collier, a working boat - the insults from the lads were, let's say...

**POSH GEORDIE MAN**: "Industrial."

**HARRY:** Aye. Racers often finished with six inches of the Tyne in their boat.

**POSH GEORDIE MAN**: Aye, and that's if you were lucky - many a competitor was capsized, sometimes by a drunken helmsman.

*Sound "ahhhhhhhhhh!" as Posh Geordie Man disappears.*

**HARRY:** Boats carrying spectators would sometimes crash into each other, hoying their passengers overboard.

*Posh Geordie appears, coughing up water.*

**POSH GEORDIE MAN**: (*coughs*) Health and safety? What's that?

**HARRY:** Aw, hadaway, man.

*Harry pushes Posh Geordie away. He disappears.*

**HARRY:** And, as a rower, getting stones hoyed at you from a bridge was a common occurrence.

*He moves front stage.*

**HARRY:** Then there were the bushes and trees ripped asunder upstream and making their way on the current to the North Sea. Not forgetting drowned sheep, cows, horses and many a bloated human corpse - oh, and trying to avoid all this when fog rolled in. And then, when your oars got broken, you're suddenly drifting downstream, helpless! And they called this "rowing for pleasure"!

*Visual: A map of North East rivers.*

**HARRY:** Races took place all over the North East: on the Tyne, from the Tyne Bar to Hexham; on the Wear; The Blyth; Talkin Tarn; the river Derwent.

*Harry is behind the lectern.*

**HARRY:** I mean, at one point there were 20 racing clubs on the Tyne alone - all racing competitively. In contrast...

**POSH MAN:** *(privileged accent)* The Henley Royal Regatta...

...which was first held in 1839 - reflected a genteel... amateur life of the upper middle class at leisure! *(silly cough and disappears).*

**HARRY:** For us working class lads, the professional game, with so much at stake, was hard and competitive.

*He moves stage front.*

**HARRY:** It was so hard that sometimes severe injury, even death occurred, especially after the final sprint in a race...the last 400 yards, when your energy's gone and muscles are screaming, and you're digging into unknown reserves - praying for the finishing bell to come.

*The finishing bell is sounded.*

**HARRY:** Ahhhhh.

*He looks at his hands, rubbing them.*

**HARRY:** Now, professional oarsmen came from the rivermen, who ferried passengers, and the keelmen, who transported goods.

Wey, man...at the start there was niy such thing as racing craft, just working boats - they were big, heavy and slow - tried and tested over centuries...

And a bugger to row.

Professionally, the Thames rivermen ruled supreme, the undisputed national champions - but us Tyne lads...we had them in our sights!

But hey, I'm rushing way ahead here - why don't we start at the beginning, eh?

*As he moves behind lectern.*

**HARRY:** A very good place to start, apparently.

*Opening bars of La Marseillaise.*

*Visuals of Napoleon.*

*1812.*

**HARRY:** The Napoleonic Wars were raging and Hartlepud – Hartelepuddle - people from Hartlepool - hung a monkey fearing it was a French spy. I mean, y'knaa, if something's hairy and has a tail it's only logical to assume it's French and hang it! Meanwhile on July the 5th in Dunston - a small village three miles upstream from Newcastle.

*Sound of baby crying "Waaa, waa".*

**HARRY:** Christened Henry, but known to everyone as

Harry. I was the second oldest boy; one of six laddies and one of 14 kids - oh aye - contraception hadn't been conceived in those days.

Well, you needed a big family to look out for each other.

Two years later...

*Stage front.*

**FATHER (V/O):** Right, we're moving.

**HARRY (AS BOY):** Where're we gannin, da?

**FATHER (V/O):** The end of the world, son.

**HARRY(AS BOY):** Jesmond?

**FATHER (V/O):** No, Jarrow!

**HARRY:** Awww, man. I loved it there. I mean, school held no attraction, though.

I was drawn to the river.

I didn't care if the Tyne was called a "cursed horse pond".

I was fascinated by the everyday life on it.

*His head follows sailing ships.*

**HARRY:** The beautiful sailing boats making their way up to Newcastle with their full-rigged sails flapping in the wind. Carrying cargoes that included tea, grain, sugar, hemp, flax, oil.

*Harry waves at distance.*

**HARRY:** (*shouts*) How, what's the name of your boat, marra?

**MAN (V/O):** Anna [Anaaaaah].

**HARRY:** Ah knaa, ye knaa, but I wanna to knaa!

**HARRY:** (*laughs to audience*) I can't believe that's still getting a laugh...the old ones are still the best, eh?

You see, this was the start of the Industrial Revolution, the era of the "Coaly Tyne" - second only in river traffic volume to the Thames.

A proper working river.

Where industry spewed out it's chemicals and assorted pollutants.

Into which butchers chucked entrails, brains, the lot, yuk.

And raw human sewage flowed.

*Harry's behind lectern.*

**HARRY:** Yuk, you wouldn't want to swim in it, I tell you, but sometimes you got pushed in.

*Sound (off) "Ahhhhhhhhhhh."*

*Sound of splash.*

*Beatrice (Geordie Woman puppet) appears holding a fishing line with a turd on the end.*

**GEORDIE WOMAN:** Eeeeeh, get them bairns oot o'that waata! And niy plodgin', wor Harry!

*The turd follows him.*

**HARRY:** Ugh, ugh - get that away from iz, man - ugh, ugh, stop following iz.

*He pushes it away. Beatrice disappears. He wipes his hands.*

*He moves to stage.*

*Visual of Jarrow Colliery.*

**HARRY:** In 1827, aged 14, I started down Jarra Pit with me fatha.

A pound a week!

Most of that went into the family pot.

Jarrow pit was notorious for methane...

*He crawls along the stage*

**HARRY:** ...a combustible and poisonous gas, or as was commonly know, firedamp.

After two weeks.

*The sound of an explosion and he's thrown to the ground.*

**HARRY:** Ahhhhhhhh.

*He stands up.*

**HARRY:** Well, I decided mining didn't suit iz.

I left, just before another explosion took 50 lives - human life came cheap...to the coal owners.

*Visual of Brown's boatyard.*

**HARRY:** Soon after I was apprenticed as a ship's carpenter at Brown's Boatyard, Jarrow, later Palmers.

I loved it.

Watching the older lads like a hawk.

*He gets a clout on the head.*

**HARRY:** Owwww!

And sometimes getting a clout ower the heed for getting things wrong. It was here I learnt so much - the basics about woodworking, the tools of the trade. And the design and construction of boats.

Wey, it was in Jarra that I first started sculling.

*He's behind lectern.*

**HARRY:** One day I was going to build my own boat!

*Posh Geordie Man appears.*

**POSH GEORDIE MAN:** By now us Tynesiders were known as Geordies.

**HARRY:** There's always been a bit of a dispute about how

the name came about.

**POSH GEORDIE MAN:** Some say it was wor allegiance to King George II in the 1745 Jacobite Uprising.

*Visual of George Stephenson.*

**HARRY:** But it most likely originates from George Stephenson.

**POSH GEORDIE MAN:** Ah, yes. Now, George, or Geordie, was a pit woorker from Wylam, alang the Tyne in Northumberland.

**HARRY:** He was illiterate until he was 18 but in 1815 he invented the miners' lamp that us miners in the Northumberland and Durham coalfields used down the pit, so pitmen got the nickname Geordies.

**POSH GEORDIE MAN:** And when in 1826, Stephenson, who was by now renowned as the "Fatha of Railways", gave evidence to a Parliamentary Commission, wey, they laughed at his accent.

**HARRY:** Here's one of the greatest minds of the day being ridiculed for the way he taaked.

**POSH GEORDIE MAN:** Ah knaa!

**HARRY:** Ah knaa ye knaa.

**POSH GEORDIE MAN:** Well get on with it.

**HARRY:** From their contemptuous sneers, these privileged snobs caalled the trimmers, lads who shovelled coal,

Geordie - and the name stuck. Aye, and we were proud to have our own language.

*Geordie Woman appears.*

**GEORDIE WOMAN:** Divent drop your dottle on the proggy mat, pet.

**POSH GEORDIE MAN:** Howay, man.

**GEORDIE WOMAN:** Ah divent knaa.

**POSH GEORDIE:** And, of course, the wonderful greeting...

**GEORDIE WOMAN:** Eeeeeeeeeee are y'alreet, hinny?

**POSH GEORDIE MAN:** Wey, I'm gannin y'hem, noo.

**HARRY:** Aye, see yous later.

*He removes puppets.*

**HARRY:** Whatever the origin, the 1830s, 40s and 50s, right up to the end of the century saw a transformation in Newcastle itself.

*Visuals of Grainger Town/Theatre Royal/Grey Street/Central Station.*

**HARRY:** The wondrous architectural delights of Grainger Town...the Theatre Royal...Grey Street...the Central Station.

We Geordies could now identify with a modern city...one of the greatest in the world!

*He's front stage.*

**HARRY:** Now, at the same time, inventions that revolutionised the world and brought society into the modern age...

*Combined visual of George Stephenson, William Armstrong and Joseph Swan.*

**HARRY:** Steam railways...

Hydraulics...

The electric light bulb and photographic advances...

...were all driven by north east-born and bred inventors...Geordies (*points*) like Stephenson, William Armstrong and Joseph Swan. Tyneside became synonymous with heavy industry and engineering, especially along the banks of the river, which was crucial for transportation.

But my time at Browns boat builders only lasted a year, though. By 1829, me fatha, now at Hetton Colliery...

*Visual of Hetton Colliery.*

**HARRY:** ...couldn't afford to continue my apprenticeship and feed the family, so I had to go back down the pit with him - I suppose you can guess why Hetton was called Le Hole.

*He takes a lump of coal from trunk.*

**HARRY:** Coal!

Ask a young 'un today what this is, they'll say "for the barbecue". It was the fuel that fired the Industrial Revolution. Coal back then, man, was very profitable - to the mine owners.

*He angrily throws the coal back into the trunk, closes lid and sits on it.*

**HARRY:** They employed us under the hated Bond system, a kind of legalised serfdom whereby we were "signed up" to a specific colliery in the April and were forced to work there for a whole year.

Working conditions were dangerous and pit disasters, claiming dozens of lives, hundreds even, were commonplace.

Wey, to the bosses, the pit ponies were more valuable than men - and better looked after!

Attempting to unionise meant instant dismissal and being blacklisted.

In April 1831, we refused to be bound like slaves…

And the miners of Northumberland and Durham went on strike to smash the bond system.

*(shouts)* Aal oot!

The Great Strike, we called it. I was 18 years old. One of the concessions we wanted was a reduction in the hours of boys working underground from 18 to 12 hours a day.

After seven weeks, we were victorious!

Then, a year later the bosses came back for revenge and starved the lads into submission - but this sense of unity was to form the backbone of the emerging working class.

I managed to get out of the pit after the Great Strike of 1831, when the family moved back to Dunston.

*Image of foundry.*

**HARRY:** Just turned 19, I was employed as a coke burner and wherryman for the Garesfield Coke Company at nearby Derwenthaugh.

As a coke burner I shovelled coal into the ovens and as a wherryman I rowed, transporting goods - both good practices for the upper body strength needed for racing.

The early 1830s saw the emergence of professional rowers - I mean, that was the dream for us Claspers. With my two brothers - wor William and Robert - we practised on the Derwenthaugh, a tributary of the Tyne.

*Visual: Cartoon of a boat and rowers which he uses to explain positions.*

**HARRY:** Our "four" comprised me as stroke (*points to stroke*) the team captain who sets the stroke rate, the length and rhythm, and decides when to hit the speed button...a stroke has to be able to feel the boat and to know what the other rowers are capable of - a team breaks at its weakest link.

(*eulogising*) Ohhhh, there's niy feeling like it, when all of us are rowing together, as one...the harmony is just so beautiful...that's when you hear the boat sing, and when your boat sings, oh man, it's like a...a...heavenly choir.

*He snaps out of his daydream.*

**HARRY:** Um, (*points to seats*) and then, Wor William, John Thompson and Robert Dinning, all rowers.

Our Robert was the coxswain (*points to position*) - he doesn't row - the coxswain sits in front of the stroke and steers. He also has a gob on him - he shouts out my orders...sorry, imparts instructions.

We wore trousers, the arse made of wear-resistant leather covered in grease to protect you from friction on the seat - still, though, boils on the bum were a major hazard.

We also got blistered hands.

We'd put our hand in cold water but if the bleb burst and got infected, well...

...and a bad back was common...and ruptured discs always a threat.

In winter we froze and in summer, wey, there was heat exhaustion and sunburn - oh, aye, there was no sun cream back then.

Still...

*Swigs from bottle.*

**HARRY:** ...alcohol helped take the pain away, though, and vinegar did the job nicely - rubbing it on, not drinking it.

Thankfully Calamine Lotion came on the market and made you smell less like fish and chips.

Oh, did I say this was enjoyable? (*laughs*).

It was...oh, yes it was.

*Takes another drink.*

**HARRY:** The Derwenthaugh Crew, they called us.

We Claspers quickly became the undisputed Champions of the Tyne - taking on and beating all-comers.

*Puts bottle down.*

**HARRY:** Now, I left the Garesfield Coke Company in 1832 and got a start with Hawks, Crawshay & Sons Ironworks.

It was on the site of what's now Gateshead Stadium.

It was there that I met the boss's daughter.

**SUSANNAH (V/O):** Hello. I'm Susannah...Susannah Hawks.

**HARRY:** I'm, um, Harry.

**SUSANNAH (V/O):** I know, we're cousins.

**HARRY:** (*to audience*) We shared two grandparents. Her side of the family had a bit of money - I was her bit of rough.

*Wedding bells and visual of All Saints Church.*

**HARRY:** In 1836 we married in All Saints Church, Newcastle. She was 19, me 24.

*He stretches to stroke her face then faces audience.*

**HARRY:** Ah, knaa what some of you are thinking, "he married his cousin!?" It was popular then, man! Queen Victoria did it, even Charles Darwin...and Billy Stevens from number 87...hang on, he married his sister!

Our wedding certificate shows I signed with a cross - so what, I was good at other things.

*Sound of baby crying. "Waaa, Waa."*

**HARRY:** Our John arrived in November of that year. Alreet, it was only two months after we tied the knot! I knaa, I knaa...but, hey, I'm a man built for speed! Wor John once asked...

**JOHN AS CHILD (V/O):** Was I conceived in wedlock, da?

**HARRY:** No, son, in Dunston.

Now, in June 1837, the 18-year-old Victoria became queen and I was to race four amateur scullers in a singles race at the Durham Regatta - wey, that was the plan!

They drew lots, actually drew lots, y'knaa, to see who would take iz oot of the race and sacrifice their own chance.

Well this bloke gets the job, doesn't he, and comes for iz...wa oars entangled.

Wey, I realised if I didn't do owt I was ganna sink!

Wey, man, I tried to pull him out of his boat...then push him away...but my boat was likely to capsize, so ah...

*He punches.*

**HARRY:** ...dunched him.

*He holds invisible oar over head.*

**HARRY:** And when I was about to land my oar on his heed I realised my boat was sinking...so I had to jump out and swim ashore.

*He "swims".*

**HARRY:** *(laughs)* The crowd loved it!

Then, later that day, when our fours team travelled to the start, some of the crowd started hoying stones at wu, forcing us to withdraw. *(beat)* Aye, it was a canny day out in Durham.

Oh, and we had a fantastic boat. The "St Agnes", it was called. I never built St Agnes - but in it, the Derwenthaugh crew were unbeatable; the fastest in the north.

Now, the rowing season lasted from the first Monday in April to the last Monday in October and 50 to 100 thousand people watched the races - oh, aye, rowers were the footballers of their day...without the dodgy haircuts, mind.

*Sound of baby crying. "Waaa, waa."*

**HARRY:** October 1838 wor Jane came along - two bairns and counting!

Industrialisation also meant unemployment...

*He goes behind lectern.*

**HARRY:** ...and, in 1839, in Newcastle alone, with its population of 54,000, there were 3,500 men out of work.

As Charles Dickens later said...

**POSH GEORDIE MAN:** *(privileged accent)* "Hard times".

**HARRY:** Eh, Charles Dickens was a Cockney.

**POSH GEORDIE MAN:** I know, I'm just acting *(coughs and laughs)*.

**HARRY:** But spending an evening watching a race on the banks of the river was, for many, a means of relaxation - and more crucially, it was free entertainment, especially in summertime.

**POSH GEORDIE MAN:** You see, the poor wanted something to cheer up their wretched existences - something to believe in.

*Posh Geordie Man disappears.*

*Harry moves to stage front.*

*Visual of the Skiff Inn.*

**HARRY:** By 1841, Susannah and me took over our first

pub, the Skiff Inn at Derwenthaugh, on the Tyne.

The first of ten pubs we ran in the next 29 years...we stayed here for eight years, until 1849, and it was ideal - a place where we could combine the licensed trade with a boatbuilding business.

Now, the first boat I built was a skiff...a small craft with two oars - called "Hawk".

*Sound of baby crying. "Waaa, waa."*

**HARRY:** September 1841. Bairn number three, Wor Ann, was born.

A year later came "Young Hawk" – that's not another bairn, it was a skiff I built - which in June 1842 won the Durham Regatta single scullers race.

I dodged the mad oarsman and stone throwers that year!

*Image of Harry posing on screen.*

**HARRY:** Another highlight that year was winning the Tyne Regatta - 10,000 people gathered on the sands at North and South Shields to cheer on the rowers.

By now, our racing team was all-Clasper, five brothers... four rowers: alongside me, wor William, Robert and Edward, and wor Richard as coxwain.

At the same time I started building a new boat, "The Five Brothers", it was to be thinner, lighter and faster.

By now every river had its champions - professional scullers who raced challengers.

On the Tyne, well, it was us, the Clasper brothers.

**HARRY:** (*shouts*) We'll race any crew, from anywhere, any time.

*Harry's behind the lectern*

**HARRY:** But the main target was to challenge the national and undisputed champions, The Thamesmen, led by the Thames champion Robert Coombes.

It was time someone knocked them off their perch.

*Cockney puppet enters.*

**COCKNEY:** (*laughs*) Are you serious?

*They eyeball each other.*

**HARRY:** Why aye - and divent look at iz like that, man!

**COCKNEY:** Do-you-speak-English?

**HARRY:** (*to audience*) I'd have knocked his block off if I wasn't just 5ft 8in – and him 6 foot.

*They eyeball each other.*

**HARRY:** I do, aye, and it's game on, bonny lad.

**COCKNEY:** Well, put your money where your mouth is, Geordie boy!

**HARRY:** (*to audience*) Now, challenge money was put up a bit like prize money for boxing. A venue, date and time for the race is agreed on

**COCKNEY:** 16th of July 1842 - we'll even come to Noocarstle.

**HARRY:** Then a purse is agreed on and sponsors are found. Now, sponsors put their money in and, after paying the crew a small percentage and expenses, take their winnings.

**COCKNEY:** Or lose their money. (*laughs*) Easy moneyyyyyy!

*Cockney Puppet disappears.*

**HARRY:** (*to Cockney*) You reckon, do you? You'll be coming to the Tyne for a ducking, bonny lad...just you wait and see.

*Posh Geordie Man appears.*

**HARRY:** (*to Posh Geordie Man*) We'll show these soft southerners who the kings of this river are, eh?

**POSH GEORDIE:** (*to audience, as an announcer*) Oyez, oyez, the race between the Tyne Crew and the London Thamesmen takes place from Newcastle Bridge...(*aside*) Now the site of the High Level Bridge.

*Visual of old Scotswood Suspension Bridge.*

**POSH GEORDIE MAN:** ...to Scotswood Suspension Bridge, Lemington. (*aside*) Now Scotswood Bridge...the one you gan over when you go to the Metro Centre.

Five miles or thereabouts...for a stake of £150 a side. (*aside*) Around £15,000 in today's money.

Oyez, oyez - God Save the Queen.

**HARRY:** (*excited*) The Thamesmen...the real Thamesmen! I thought about using my new boat, the Five Brothers...

**POSH GEORDIE MAN:** The Five Brothers? (*laughs*) Ha! It's ower flimsy

**HARRY:** It's not, man.

*Posh Geordie Man talks in his ear.*

**POSH GEORDIE MAN:** It'll sink.

**HARRY:** No it won't.

**POSH GEORDIE MAN:** Wey, it'll get blown away in the wind! Look, it's not manly enough, man.

**HARRY:** (*debates to himself*) St Agnes...or Five Brothers?

*Posh Geordie Man talks in his ear.*

**POSH GEORDIE MAN:** The St Agnes is tried and tested, stick with that, son!

*Posh Geordie Man disappears.*

**HARRY:** St Agnes...or Five Brothers...St Agnes...or Five Brothers...come on, you want to win, Harry...which one? Ah, bollocks, the St Agnes!

*Pathe News and music. Cock sounds.*

*He comes stage front, amazed at what's happening, the crowds etc.*

**MALE PATHE (V/O):** It's Sunday, July 16, 1842. Bells ring out to proclaim the match. And it looks like the whole of Tyneside has turned out to cheer on their team, led by Harry Clasper.

**REPORTER (V/O):** Excuse me, sir, what does this race mean to you?

**MAN 1 (V/O):** These Londoners take wor coal for their big hooses.

**REPORTER (V/O):** And you, madam.

**WOMAN (V/O):** Hadaway and shite!

*Harry limbers up his shoulders and arms.*

**HARRY:** Unfamiliar faces convulse the town, all with Geordie pride; the blast of the furnace is unheard and the sound of the forge has died.

Counting houses, academic seats, them with money to spend; have shut their desks and closed their doors...all social classes attend.

Newcastle Bridge full to bursting, will it take the weight? Steamers sailing on the Tyne, groan under their living freight.

Cab wheels rattle on granite roads and narrow lanes cram with people; a human throng on each bank of the Tyne...they've even climbed All Saints steeple.

*Harry takes his seat on the chest.*

*Pistol shot and cheers.*

*He rows a few strokes.*

**MAN 2 (V/O):** (*shouts*) Howay lads, hadaway Harry.

**MALE PATHE (V/O):** A deafening cheer greets the first dip of the oars.

*The cheering noise fades.*

**HARRY:** The lads gave their all but it was obvious from early on we couldn't compete with the Thames crew.

*Harry sits on the chest, dejected.*

**PATHE (V/O):** The Londoners were soon in the lead and pulled away to gain an easy victory.

**COCKNEY (V/O):** Upstarts!

**HARRY:** We rowed out the remaining four miles, deflated. The words "arses" and "kicked" spring to mind. I'd let down not just Tyneside, but the whole North East.

My people.

They dream through me.

*Harry's pensive - he's approached by Susannah. He puts his hand on his shoulder.*

**HARRY:** (*to Susannah*) Oh, hello, pet

What? Just thinking...trying to get me head straight, y'knaa

I know...I know, man

But -

Back to basics? But it's taken ten years to get here, man!

Look, it's all well and good to say come back stronger but -

Aye, well, you know I want to be world champion! (*revelation*) Of course! That's it...that's it...that's bloody well it!

*He stands.*

**HARRY:** (*to audience*) We weren't beaten by rowing...we were beaten by the *construction* of the St Agnes. Now, I studied the Londoners' boat. Theirs weighed only 160 lbs, ours was 256. Every pound of extra weight is an additional burden on the muscles of the lads - we were giving them 96 lbs - over six and a half stone!

I looked at the Five Brothers again - I was sure it could revolutionise racing craft. My intention wasn't to copy the London boat but to improve on it.

Once the pub was shut and the bairns were settled, with Susannah's help, we worked late evenings on it.

Oh aye, not only did she teach me to read and write, she was a dab hand with the old tape measure.

For six months I hammered out designs and models to upgrade the Five Brothers. Faster racing boats have to be lighter and smaller so there's less drag and friction.

*Visuals of the Five Brothers design.*

**HARRY:** What if...what if, we put the keel inside the hull with a single plank on each side to cut down friction?

And then varnished the hull to cut even more friction?

But that's not all.

What if we used outriggers as a frame that holds the rowlock? *(to audience)* The rowlock is the socket that the oar slots into.

Not only did the outrigger improve holding the oars in place, it allowed the rowers to swing a longer oar, and more pull meant...

more speed.

It also gave the rowers greater control of the craft.

It was a revolution in boat design.

When we unveiled the Five Brothers in 1843 there was a gasp! *(beat, to audience)* Howay, you're supposed to gasp - let's try again!

*He goes behind the lectern.*

**HARRY:** When we unveiled the Five Brothers in 1843, there was a gasp!

[GASP]

**HARRY:** Better!

*Posh Geordie Man appears.*

**POSH GEORDIE MAN:** Well, I've seen nowt like it...it looks like a floating toothpick! And what's with the scooped oar?

**HARRY:** Wey, we'd used a straight oar against the Thamesmen but theirs was scooped, which gave them an advantage.

We also developed what became known as the "Tyne Stroke" - sliding on the fixed seats, using wa legs to produce a longer, more powerful stroke.

All except wor Edward, of course, who had a wooden leg, which he took off in the boat. I used to kid him on that the only reason he's included is that he makes the boat lighter. (*laughs*).

(*solemnly*) Ah, Edward - you know, when he first started rowing he asked why was it that Oxford and Cambridge always get to the final of the boat race. (*beat, excited*). Anyway, that season, in the Five Brothers, us Claspers were unbeatable on the Tyne.

It was time to take on the Cockneys again.

**POSH GEORDIE MAN:** June 1844 - The Royal Thames Regatta.

**HARRY:** Hold on, man...

We had to get there first. (*shouts*) All aboard The Innisfail, all aboard.

*Sound of steam ship horn.*

**HARRY:** It was a steam ship, and London was a long way away.

*Posh Geordie Man gives directions.*

**POSH GEORDIE MAN:** London? Phew! I'd say gan doon the Tyne, past Jarra Slake (*pronounced slack*) to Sooth Shields. Then turn left, no, no, right, aye definitely take a right, past the Marsden Grotto pub, past Sunderland...

Past Hartlepool - but divent taak French there, mind - and straight on for, phooor (*breaths out*) two days?

*Posh Geordie Man disappears.*

**HARRY:** The Five Brothers was in the hold and we kept an eye on it throughout - with such high stakes, it wasn't unusual to find holes drilled into your boat - have you ever heard of the word "skul-duggery"?

*Cockney Puppet appears.*

**COCKNEY:** (*sings*) Knees up Mother Brown, Knees up Mother Brown, oy!

*Visual of Nelson's Column being constructed.*

**HARRY:** (*in awe, looking around*) So this is London, eh? I'd heard of an author from here - what the Dickens is his name?

The Thamesmen, hearing about our advances, had slimmed down their boats too. Despite the Five Brothers being much lighter than the St Agnes, she was still about 20 per cent heavier than the boats being raced on the Thames. But they'd never seen owt like it, shapewise.

*Cockney looks over lectern at the Five Brothers' image.*

**HARRY:** Hey!

**COCKNEY:** (*laughs*) It'll be impossible to row her steadily because she's shaped like a gun barrel...and what's this, outriggers like that? (*laughs*) Stupid Geordies.

*Cockney Puppet disappears.*

**HARRY:** Let them laugh, lads, it's easier to race against a crew you don't like.

**ANNOUNCER (V/O):** Ladies and gentlemen, welcome to the 1844 Royal Thames Regatta.

*A starting gunshot and cheers.*

**HARRY:** We easily won the £50 prize in the heats. The Cockneys weren't laughing any more.

*Posh Puppet Appears.*

**POSH MAN:** The Newcastle men have a stroke peculiar to themselves. Their extraordinary boat and beautiful rowing has rendered them objects of considerable interest.

**ANNOUNCER (V/O):** Ladies and gentlemen, we now come to the final of the Champion Fours for a prize of

£100 and the title "Champions of the world".

*Gunshot sound.*

*Cheers and sound of "hadaway Harry, hadaway lads" as Harry comes front stage and sits, crestfallen.*

*The cheering fades.*

**HARRY:** It wasn't to be our year, though. The Five Brothers suffered a broken pin on only the second stroke. So Coombes' crew won easily. Another factor was our Richard's inexperience on the Thames. Not knowing the fastest water and giving ground to the other boats...as our cox, he'd caused a navigational error.

He was inconsolable.

*Harry stands.*

**HARRY:** (*to Richard, ruffles his hair*) Hey, hey, howay...don't worry, bonny lad...the boat's new, it had steering problems. (*to audience*) But was it the boat or was it was us?

(*stares out at audience*) Next year, Richard.

This time next year - we'll be the champions of the world.

### END OF ACT ONE

# ACT TWO

*Blackout.*

**COMMENTATOR (OFF):** After the disappointment of not being able to contend in the Champion's Prize, the committee got up a purse of £40 to be rowed for by the Clasper crew against the Coombes' crew.

*Cheering.*

**COMMENTATOR (OFF):** It was oar to oar but then the Tynemen drew away.

**V/O:** Howay Harry, hadaway lads.

**COMMENTATOR (OFF):** The cheering was deafening...we could hear Geordie voices everywhere.

**V/O:** Howay lads, hadaway Harry.

*Cheering stops.*

**COMMENTATOR (OFF):** The Tynemen won in eight and a half minutes - a time usually recorded by an eight-oared boat!

They were magnificent!

*Lights up, Harry enters, as if after a race, arms up in victory.*

**HARRY:** We'd arrived! It might have been unofficial but the Tynemen had well and truly arrived!

A month later...

*A baby cries "Waaa, waa."*

**HARRY:** So had bairn number four! Wor Elizabeth...keep counting!

*He goes behind lectern.*

**HARRY:** I won another five races that year in London and Newcastle. But I really wanted to take on the Thames Champion, Robert Coombes, in a one on one.

*Cockney Puppet appears.*

**COCKNEY:** From Newcaarstle Bridge to Scotswood Suspension Bridge - a distance of five miles or thereabouts...oy!

**HARRY:** It was a race all Tyneside was waiting for - the Champions of the Tyne and Thames competing. Wey man, I could hardly get from one end of the street to the other.

**GEORDIE MAN (V/O):** Beat him, Harry!

*Geordie Woman puppet appears.*

**GEORDIE WOMAN:** Eeeeeeh, good luck, Harry!

*She kisses him.*

**HARRY:** Alright!

*He comes stage front.*

**HARRY:** Both boats were built specially for the race. Coombes' weighed 43lb, mine 49 - a six pound difference.

*He sits on chest, limbering up and then concentrating.*

**HARRY:** December 18. Race day.

**COMMENTATOR (V/O):** All vantage points are taken as tens of thousands defy the freezing cold and turn out for this race.

People are betting on the outcome.

The noise is unbearable.

And they're...

*Gunfire.*

**COMMENTATOR (V/O):** ...off!

**CROWD (V/O):** Hadaway Harry.

**COMMENTATOR (V/O):** Matching stroke for stroke.

*Crowd cheering.*

*He rows.*

**HARRY:** I had him in my peripheral vision - but from the off he kept coming over to iz. (*shouts left*) Steer straight...steer straight...get oot the way, man, get oot the way.

I move on the inside, so he turns inside, forcing iz out wider...get out me bloody way, will you! I go even wider but he still follows iz. (*shouts left*) Get oot the way, man...get out!

Then tragedy struck, didn't it? A keelboat hit iz...bang!

*He falls aside and stops rowing.*

**HARRY:** The oar gets knocked from my grip. By the time I recover, he's gone four lengths up.

Momentum gone.

To get my boat back up to speed is well nigh impossible. That's when the crowd - 100,000 people - go quiet, an eerie silence descends - you don't just sense, you *feel* their intense disappointment, their despondency.

Then the belief goes.

And the moment you think you've lost it, you have.

*He stands.*

**HARRY:** Pride punctured, my eyes well up. Every worthless stroke to the finishing line is grudgingly rowed. (*holds nose*) And Clasper trails in by six boat lengths.

*He's behind lectern.*

**HARRY:** That's the defining moment - you either walk away, or you're determined you'll never feel that humiliation again.

*Cockney Puppet appears.*

**COCKNEY:** Oy, Geordie, thay say I forced you to collide with a keel boat.

**HARRY:** No. You beat iz fair and square.

**COCKNEY:** Good. Do you, eh, fancy a rematch next week?

**HARRY:** Definitely.

**COCKNEY:** Ha. In your dreams! (*laughs*) Happy New Year (*in Geordie*) Harry.

**HARRY:** Aye, happy New Year...Robert.

*He comes front stage.*

**HARRY:** (*up-beat*) January 1845 - all eyes were on the Championship of the World at the Thames Regatta in June. And the Clasper brothers' names were going to be on that cup.

Right lads, listen up. If we want to be champions, wa ganna have to train like champions.

*Takes off shirt (he's wearing a vest) and puts on heavy overcoat from trunk.*

**HARRY:** Rule number one - never underestimate your opponent - the training regime will be as follows:

*Cock crows.*

**HARRY:** 6.30am. Out of bed, and warm-up exercises.

*Does sit ups.*

**HARRY:** 6.45am. A gentle walk for five miles - wearing a heavy overcoat.

*Walks/marches.*

**HARRY:** 8am. Breakfast - a mutton chop or two fresh eggs, washed down with a cup of tea - never coffee...yum!

9am. A smart run - wearing a heavy overcoat.

*Runs on spot and punches forward.*

**HARRY:** 10am. Enter boat for the morning row.

*Rows.*

**HARRY:** 11am. An hour's rest.

Mid-day. Dinner time...beef or mutton broiled on the gridiron followed by a light egg pudding...one glass of ale and a glass of port wine...or two glasses of ale without the wine.

1pm. Back in the boats for a hard row.

*Rows.*

**HARRY:** 3pm. Wearing an excess of clothing (*shows overcoat*) put to bed to sweat.

*Lies down.*

**HARRY:** 4pm. Undressed to be rubbed down and left to cool down.

*Gets up.*

**HARRY:** 5pm. Meal three of the day - tea and toast...sparingly buttered with only one egg - more than that chokes the system.

Then rest.

9pm. If you want supper this will be new milk and bread - or gruel with raisins and currants...and one, I mean one, glass of port wine.

10pm. Bed.

*He stretches and yawns.*

**HARRY:** Any problems?

Good.

Any questions?

Yes Edward! (*beat*) No we can't gan to the pub!

Well done lads.

Oh, and don't forget to grease your arses.

(*to audience*) You see, prize rowing isn't just a sport, it's a way of life. For the next six months we entered a liquid world.

A world in which your stinking training gear would never

dry...sweat-drenched socks, jumpers, trousers, shoes, hats, gloves.

A world of frosted breath, where ice collects on your hair and shoulders as the winter rain and snow penetrates your every pore and freezes you to the marrow - despite your exertions.

A world of white, wrinkled and numb hands, arms numb to the elbow and feet cracking with pain.

**MAN OFF:** (*painful*) Ahhhhhhhh.

**HARRY:** That's the sound of someone freezing cold taking a hot bath. (*shouts*) Hey, shut up, Edward!

A world in which morning is still in moonlight and you finish your training in the dark.

A world in which you miss birthdays, wedding anniversaries...and an understanding better half is essential.

We trained hard for six months...a team, four rowers as one.

Endless hours - all day, every day and weekends, in all weather - covering thousands of miles in the boat, understanding its surge and flow.

Defining improvements...small, incremental but vital improvements, and constantly setting new goals.

Four rowers as one.

But we needed a new boat.

We got...the Lord Ravensworth.

Fitted with v-shaped outriggers, it was narrower, lighter...

And faster.

Oh, man, even if I say it myself, it was finest boat ever built.

Yessssssss - we were going to make this boat sing - we are going to be world champions!

*The death knell sounds.*

**HARRY:** April 1, 1845.

What?

It can't be.

No, no! (*upset*) Please no...why?

**CLERGYMAN (V/O):** Ashes to ashes, dust to dust.

**HARRY:** Edward... me little brother, me crew mate, me, me...marra...he was only 25 years old.

*He's upset and responds to a hand on his shoulder.*

**HARRY:** Oh, hello, pet I've told them. I've told the lads we'll not be going to London this year.

Well, even if I was in the right frame of mind, how do you replace Edward? (*beat*) What!?

Uncle Ned?! That beer on your apron's gone to your heed...are you serious?

Look, I know Ned was a canny rower in his time but...well, he old! He's 42! (*to audience*) Given the average age of death was 37 for men and 36 for women, this was old!

And you can understand why the marriage vows included "till death do us part".

Where were we? Oh aye, owld Ned (*points*) There he was...doing press ups on one hand!

He'd already got to 100 withoot a sweat on!

Right, em, that's it, then...the, eh, owld 'un's in!

*Sound and visual of steam train.*

**HARRY:** Now, this time we travelled to London by train - we'd heard tales of sparks from train engines setting fire to boats strapped to the roof so we kept an eye on the Lord Ravensworth - in the guard's van

*Sings Lambeth Walk in Cockney and struts to lectern.*

(*sings*) Anytime you're Lambeth way, any evening, any day, you'll find us all doin' the Lambeth walk...oy!

*Cockney Puppet appears.*

**HARRY:** This time we weren't in awe of London. As it turned out, people were in awe of us!

**COCKNEY:** Awl royt, Geordie?

**HARRY:** Aal reet.

*Cockney looks over lectern at image of the Lord Ravensworth.*

**HARRY:** And not just us, but the Lord Ravensworth as well

Hey! Niy touching!

**COCKNEY:** (*to audience*) Would you Adam and Eve it, ay?

*Cockney disappears.*

**ANNOUNCER (V/O)**: And please, a warm Thames Regatta welcome for the Tyne crew, led by Mr Harry Clasper.

*Applause.*

*Harry, stage front, waves.*

**HARRY:** We got through the two heats easily enough and now we were in the final...the championship of the world - against two London crews. One led by Bob Newell...(*nods left*) The other...led by my old adversary Robert Coombes (*nods right*)

*He moves to chest and puts on his rowing top.*

**HARRY:** Well, this is it, lads - cast your minds back to January, those dark, cold days when this was a distant dream - this is what you've put in the sacrifice for.

And remember, they have the home crowd, so they'll keep coming back at us. (*energetic*) Are we ready? (*beat*) Good - gan to the netty first!

*Visual: Route map of race Putney to Chiswick Eyot.*

**PATHE MAN (V/O):** The Thames presented a scene of gaiety unprecedented as to excite universal admiration.

*Harry puts his towel around him and drinks from a bottle.*

**PATHE MAN (V/O):** Myriads of persons, both on water and on shore, awaited with feverish impatience along all 2.5 miles from the start at Putney Bridge to the finish at Chiswick Oyet.

**ANNOUNCER (V/O):** Start lining up gentlemen, please.

**PATHE MAN (V/O):** Would the London watermen retain their well-earned laurels as champions of the world or yield them to the gallant and enterprising men of the Tyne?

**GEORDIE MAN (V/O):** Hadaway Harry, hadaway lads.

*Harry salutes them.*

**HARRY:** The Geordies in London had turned up en masse from the docks to cheer us on. The noise was deafening. We knew exactly why we were here.

*Cheering.*

*Harry waves as he comes stage front, kneels, looks out and around and pours water over his head from bottle.*

**GEORDIE MAN (V/O):** Gan on Harry!

*He mops up water with towel, waves and sits on trunk.*

**ANNOUNCER (V/O):** Line up chaps, that's good.

**HARRY:** The clear, unpolluted water of Putney contrasted starkly with the brown, smelly sludge of the Tyne. Oh, the beautiful Tyne; she might be dirty but she was ours - and we were going to make her proud.

We'd been drawn in the middle, with Coombes on the advantageous inside. We'd have to cut them off before the all-important Surrey Bend. The leader there generally wins.

My heart's pounding. I'm sure Coombes's crew can hear it even above the din. They share a joke...is it confidence or bravado?

I look back for reassurance...wor William, wor Robert and Uncle Ned. I wink to appear relaxed. They smile back sheepishly and grip their oars.

Wor Richard, crouched like a jockey in front, a lesson in concentration...will he navigate us successfully this time? I know the experience of last year still haunts him.

He catches my eye, pats my shoulder and smiles. I grab his leg in acknowledgement. The adrenaline surges. I get a boost of much-needed confidence.

Putney Bridge just behind us is crammed with thousands of people, all shouting and waving. I want to say "right lads, remember, we're running our own race – controlled and disciplined" but there's no point, it's too late for a team talk.

We're in our start positions now.

Legs and arms bent, hands clasping the oar.

Back straight. Ready to go.

*Crowd noises.*

**HARRY:** We're only eight and a half minutes away from the dream.

**ANNOUNCER (V/O):** Are you ready?

**HARRY:** (*shouts*) for Edward!

**ANNOUNCER (V/O):** Attention-

**HARRY:** Hey! (*to audience*) The Coombes crew pull out early.

*Gun fires.*

**HARRY:** The crowd erupts.

*Crowd noises.*

**HARRY:** Richard bellows (*shouts*) draw. The first stroke, that all-important first stroke - no ripping, don't rip it, lads - just take up the pressure and press long. (*shouts*) Go!

*Harry rows from here to the end of the race.*

**HARRY:** I squeeze the blades into the water ... every moment feels like an eternity...the boat moves...it's smooth...it's a good start.

A race can be won or lost in the first minute, that initial sprint - everyone must be in it together.

We kick in at over 50 strokes a minute...the pain soon

builds, we're all taking short and deep breaths.

Coombes's boat comes closer to our side looking for faster water...we need to hold the main line of the stream, the middle's where the water's deepest and the current the fastest.

Richard steers us straight, he's not giving an inch this time.

All three boats are together, matching stroke for stroke. (*shouts*) Rhythm, hold.

After 400 yards, I drop the rate of striking to 45, we enter our race rhythm - and glide further between each stroke. It's a marginally more sustainable pace, preserving vital energy for when it's needed. The steamers moored at Putney Embankment fly by and we soon leave the euphoria of Putney Bridge behind.

Stroke for stroke - all three crews are in tandem.

The crowds cheer, their detail becomes less and less defined as sweat fills my eyes...only their noise can be heard above the sound of our oars dipping into the rough water stretch as we pass Fulham on our left-hand side, and head towards Hammersmith.

The summer wind blows against the incoming flow of the tide...water from the blades sprays across us but the rhythm, it feels good.

**COMMENTATOR (V/O):** Half a mile gone and Coombes's crew are beginning to inch ahead.

**HARRY:** Just opposite the Craven Cottage, Coombes takes

the lead - only half a length up but if they break clear now they'll be hard to catch, especially if they get the inside on Surrey Bend - but that's a mile away and we're oar to oar with Newell.

They come too close...(*shouts*) How, man, bugger off.

Richard steers us...again, he's still not giving an inch.

I call on the lads...(*shouts*) Up strokes!

Hu, hu, hu.

We lift ourselves from the already painful rhythm to a faster one...it works. We're soon a seat up on Newell and quickly move away to three-quarters of a length - Coombes is nearby, just ahead, I can hear their cox urging them on.

I call on ten big strokes.

In two, in one (*shouts*) ten full!

Hu, hu, hu.

The surge of power is unbelievable as all four of us commit our full strength.

We take off...I can sense Ned's frame shaking with the full force he's sending down...we begin to leave Newell behind...another 200 yards...we ease off slightly.

We're tailing Coombes by half a length. It's good though...they know we're there...they can hear us...let them feel the heat.

The Crabtree pub is coming up on our left.

We're just past half way. Richard shouts:

**RICHARD (V/O):** (*shouts*) Big push at Crabtree.

**COMMENTATOR (V/O):** And the men of the Thames are edging the Tynemen.

**HARRY:** In two, in one (*shouts*) twenty full!

Hu, hu, hu.

This time 20 big ones are unleashed and we're pressing coombes.

I catch him out of the corner of my eye. He's digging in now. He looks up and we glance, momentarily...at that moment he's my enemy and I detest him.

**COMMENTATOR (V/O):** And the Tyne team are level with Coombes.

**HARRY:** Two hundred yards later, I call on the lads again.

In two, in one, (*shouts*) twenty more!

Hu, hu, hu.

Another power surge and we're edging ahead.

All the time I'm wondering how much Coombes' crew have in them. They'll have been training in the cold winter months for this an'all.

Never underestimate your opponent.

We could have overtaken them there but with just under a mile to go it was too early to make for home - I wanted us to have enough in the tank for that final burst.

**COMMENTATOR (V/O):** In response the Coombes crew up their stroke.

**HARRY:** Bugger!

**COMMENTATOR (V/O):** Both boats fly under Hammersmith Suspension Bridge - 12,000 people on the edifice are cheering and stomping as the rowers pass below.

**HARRY:** Surrey Bend's up ahead...that all-important Surrey Bend (*shouts*) Ten.

Ten big strokes through the bridge - then out into the wide expanse of the Thames.

There's dozens of boats on either side, crammed with spectators. A deafening roar goes up as the crowd get their first view of us emerging from under the bridge.

I call another (*shouts*) ten.

And we're pulling away from Coombes...only inches per stroke but it's enough

We pull half a length ahead.

It soon becomes a length and they're in full view behind us.

I see their oars splashing into the water...their cox shouting for more effort.

Newell's crew fall even further back further - it's between us and Coombes now.

Two hundred yards to the long, meandering Surrey Bend and the two-mile marker...we're still a length up.

Six minutes in, most races are decided by now.

What have they got left?

Never ever underestimate your opponent.

Richard sees the Surrey Bend and shouts:

**RICHARD (V/O):** (*shouts*) Defend the bend, defend the bend.

**HARRY:** It's worth a length at least if we make them work harder on the outside.

I call again (*shouts*) twenty.

Richard is animated, screaming out instructions.

**RICHARD (V/O):** Pull...legs, legs, sit up, sit up, pull, pull.

**HARRY:** My beautiful lads respond with twenty of the biggest strokes of our lives...the feeling is indescribable, I get tingles down my spine.

But it only serves to encourage Coombes' crew, who start to creep up on the inside.

Richard turns the rudder to cut into them - forcing them off their line. I look at him, he winks...the naughty bastard!

Richard imparts more instructions.

**RICHARD (V/O):** *(shouts)* Spring off, spring off.

**HARRY:** I call for another ten. The lads respond again... we're that all-important length ahead.

Richard steers us to the inside of the bend.

He wants more from us.

**RICHARD (V/O):** *(shouts)* Move it.

**HARRY:** I call again *(shouts)* ten.

The lads respond again.

The boat feels like it sprouted wings...we cut inside...it's magnificent, truly magnificent.

We've got the Surrey side...we've got the inside! Oh, you beauty, Richard!

We force Coombes to come on the outside, they lose valuable ground and energy.

We all lean even more weight on the oar and push our legs harder.

We're keeping tight on the bend...they're pushing on again, straining to keep up with us.

We concede no ground but every time I force my legs down harder, the pain increases, my arms ache more.

Still holding the bend...on our right is St Paul's School...we're two lengths up now...hold them here and we've won...Robert, pumping away behind, knows it. He lets out an encouraging scream and we all send down even harder strokes.

We come out of the bend - it's rough water but straight again.

Two lengths ahead...Richard nods, he can see the green island of Chiswick Eyot ahead in the distance.

But never, ever underestimate your opponent.

It's 600 yards away...only 600 yards to the finishing line.

This is our chance to move further ahead...we've planned to break them here.

I look at Richard and nod. He screams:

**RICHARD (V/O):** (*shouts*) Edward!

**HARRY:** It's the final signal.

Four voices echo him (*shouts*) Edward!

Twenty huge power strokes. I'm counting down inside, nineteen, eighteen, seventeen...I know the others will be too.

Four pistons work harder to increase the speed.

Boat and crew as one.

Perfect harmony.

Surging between strokes.

This is what it's all aboot!

**COMMENTATOR (V/O):** And the Tyne crew have increased their lead to two and a half lengths.

**HARRY:** Whatever Coombes's crew have left, they've got to throw it at us now - their final push, it has to be! We've got them on the ropes. You hope they've got nothing...surely they'll crumble now - they can't keep up with us.

But they push again, moving slowly but steadily back on us...we're now only two lengths ahead. (*shouts*) Ten.

More power strokes, we push them back again...but they just keep coming.

I hear ear-splitting screams - cheers and boos rise from the bank to almost deafen us.

They're gaining on us...they must be gaining on us.

We dig our oars in against the pull of the current and every muscle strains with the load

We take long strokes...we're still together...our oars cut into the Thames, gripping the water more effectively.

I've seen these lads in training, giving their all, I envisaged

Robert gritting his teeth and William, mouth agape, searching for breath, pumping his arms - but this is the real thing...how much have we left?

To my left, I see Coombes coming back into contention.

Our pace isn't slacking, though - the lads are pulling their hearts out, stroke after stroke after stroke.

Four brothers and Ned willing to sacrifice everything for this race. Id never been so proud of these boys.

The rowing's smooth, powerful and flowing...hypnotic.

Four of us as one.

Sweat drips and stings, blurring vision.

But now, Coombes' bow comes level with our stern. We're only a length ahead.

I move the stroke rate up again - I worry whether the lads'll respond this time. (*shouts*) Ten.

I hear three "howay lads" in different groans – Ned sounds the weakest...the lads are coming with me, though...(*excited*) they're coming with me...and the old boy's still hanging in there – please don't falter Ned.

My heart lifts with every stroke, we inch further ahead. Our big moves have worked...it's beautiful...we can do this...we can do this.

I want to shout out "listen lads, can you hear it? It's singing...the boat's singing!"

But I'm too exhausted.

*Richard gets animated and points.*

**RICHARD (V/O):** (*screams*) Cheswick Eyot, Harry, Cheswick Eyot.

**HARRY:** 250 yards to go. I summon up the final ounces of my energy. (*shouts*) Go!

The final sprint, we're back up to 50 strokes.

Two hundred yards. My lungs feel as if they're filled with acid. I taste blood - I'm on the verge of passing out. I'm searching for breath...pumping my arms...it only needs one of us to crack and it's game over.

But we're all as one - no-one daring to let the side down. Pain surges through my body. I'm searching for oxygen with short rapid breaths. My heart's thumping in my chest.

**RICHARD (V/O):** 30 seconds. Pull, pull.

**HARRY:** I hear Richard demanding more from the lads.

Our oars tear the water into lumps of foam.

The pain's blinding.

My heart's pounding, at over 200 beats a minute this is heart attack territory - but you can't take it easy or catch your breath.

A boxer could go down at this stage but there's nowhere to hide in a boat.

Stay together lads.

**RICHARD (V/O):** 29...28.

**HARRY:** His voice seemed to float away - we're two lengths up and in our heads we're all counting down...27...26.

Belief runs through the crew...each and every one of them fighting their own inner battle for the greater good.

25...24...

Then I hear their cox..."more power". He's getting louder and louder, screaming (*loud*) "more power, more power".

They're gaining.

The rhythmic sound of their oars...they try to finish us.

There's silence but we communicate without words...all putting in similar huge effort, not wanting to let the side down.

23...22...21...

They haven't taken any advantage.

Fewer calls come from inside their boat...they're now deep in pain territory.

**RICHARD (V/O):** (*shouts*) Stay together.

**HARRY:** Richard's voice calms us.

The rhythmic thump of their finishes gets less pronounced.

They're tiring, they have to be.

**RICHARD (V/O):** (*shouts*) 50 yards...take it home, lads - up two.

**HARRY:** Up two! I can't!

I'm already sending down everything I have. Above the din I can hear Ned gasping in loud croaks, there's nothing left in his tank...only the burning desire not to let us down is driving him past breaking point.

Keep going, Ned, please keep going.

Dig deep, lads, dig deep...but I'm now too far gone - my legs scream "no more", my lungs beg for mercy and my head feels as if it's about to explode.

The mind, it's now all in the mind - will it be strong enough to keep pushing on or will it break?

How much do you want this Harry? How much, do you want it?

18...17...16...

*The crowd noise stops.*

**HARRY:** I no longer hear the screaming crowd, darkness is descending.

My body screams *(loud)* STOP!

*His rowing is out, distorted.*

**HARRY:** *(He's disorientated, emotional)* Uh, uh...then suddenly the rowing's no longer in sync. *(panicking)* The boat feels loose. Why have we stopped racing?

I look back. Ned's head's dropped, his hands by his sides, he's slumped forward...motionless.

I try to shout "Ned"...but nothing comes out.

I see wor Robert flopped over his oar, desperately gasping for air.

William lies back on Robert's lap, his chest bellowing as he groans and sucks in oxygen.

What's happened?

I try to swallow. I can't. All my senses have stop working.

Why did we throw the race away so close to home?

And then Richard leans forward and kisses iz on the forehead.

**RICHARD (V/O):** We won, Harry, we won! We're the champions of the world!

**HARRY:** *(beat)* I see he's bawling his eyes out. He's always been a soft shite.

Tears well up in my eyes and I cry...like a little bairn...tears of joy flood down my cheeks...I cry uncontrollably. I muster all my strength to look behind again. Through the veil of tears, I see wor Ned - eyes rolled back into his head, chest heaving, groaning, frantically trying to suck oxygen into his gasping mouth.

Robert, arm on the gunwale, is gasping for air. He's ashen...as white as a ghost. He looks up and stares at iz, eyes vacant from fatigue, he tries to smile, but his bottom lip just trembles.

I try to communicate but nothing happens. Wor William...now bent forward, being sick. Between retches he groans - but he's alive.

Knowing the lads are safe, I slump forward for what felt like an eternity, but it must have only been a few seconds. I try to remember the last fifty yards but they're a complete blank.

As my senses return, I see people...the sheer number is overwhelming...the banks have erupted...hats are being waved and thrown in the air. Those who aren't clapping and cheering are pointing.

(*To lads*) Hey lads...lads...look, they're pointing at us.

*Visual of rowing crowd cheering.*

**ANNOUNCER (V/O):** And the winners, by a length and a half...the Tyneside crew.

Three cheers! Hip, hip, hooray!

**HARRY:** Those of us who aren't vomiting or passing out manage a feeble wave (*feeble wave*) hooray.

I look up at wor Richard. I say: "Shoot me if I ever gan near a boat again".

He laughs. Then someone puts a bottle of champagne in my hand.

*He swigs from the bottle.*

**HARRY:** The liquid tastes wet...and wonderful.

Hey lads *(waves bottle)* if they could see us back home now... we'd be disowned! But the taste of victory is every bit as sweet as I imagined it would be.

**COMMENTATOR (V/O):** Sir Lancelot Shadwell, Vice Chancellor of England, will make the presentation.

**SHADWELL (V/O):** Although the winners were Tyne men, the London watermen did not find them "tin-y" competitors *(laughs, snorts)*.

**HARRY:** He actually said that – "tin-y competitors" - and even laughed at his own joke!

*He laughs as he dries his face with the towel.*

*Mood changes to post Putney.*

**HARRY:** We were nicknamed the "Famous Five" – long before Enid Blyton came on the scene.

*He waves towel and salutes the crowd.*

*Bell rings out.*

**HARRY:** Church bells rang out in Newcastle and Gateshead to greet our return. Huge crowds turned out to welcome us...tens of thousands. People, as far as the eye could see. There were flags and bunting everywhere. The guns at Hawks & Crawshays' works were fired in salute.

*Gun blast.*

**MAN (OFF):** Ahhhhhhhhh!

**HARRY:** That's probably someone falling out of a pub.

Away from the rowing, me and the lads were celebrities. All sorts of memorabilia: cups, plates, post cards, ink wells, lockets and statues were created.

*Visual of Harry standing/posing.*

**HARRY:** We had our portraits painted and photographs taken.

*He smooths hair and poses similar to photo image.*

**HARRY:** We were celebrated in newspapers and music halls. Numerous songs were written and performed - like this by J.P. Robson.

*Music "Harry Clasper" by J P Robson.*

**HARRY:** (*Sings*) "Ov a' your grand rowers in skiff or in scull, there's nyen wi' wor Harry has chance for to pull.

Man, he sits like a duke an' he fetches so free
Oh! Harry's the lad, Harry Clasper for me!

Hadaway, Harry! Canny lad Harry!
Harry's the king of the Thames an' the Tyne" *(fades)*.

Aye, well I'm a rower, not a singer.

*Harry takes off his top and stares at it lovingly before putting it into the trunk and changing into the narrator's clothes (kept in the shoulder bag).*

**NARRATOR:**  In July, Harry celebrated his 33rd birthday. And at the North of England regatta won the fours and the singles.

Thomas Carroll, Champion of the Mersey, challenged Harry to a race in Liverpool on September 29, 1845, for a prize of £200. Tens of thousands converged for the race.

The Newcastle and Carlisle Railway Company even put on a special excursion train to bring our people cross country to see the race.

Harry beat him by 300 yards-plus.

Carroll's excuse?

*(Scouse)* I had boils on me bum, you know.

In November Harry beat William Pocock, the Thames Champion, in Newcastle for £100 a side.

Historians might say 1845 was the epitome of Harry's peak as an oarsman, a boat designer and builder and trainer.

They wouldn't be far wrong.

*He's now changed back into the modern narrator.*

**NARRATOR:** After becoming world champions in 1845, Harry's design was taken up nationally. It became the norm in racing boats.

And still is today.

*He goes behind lectern.*

**NARRATOR:** For the next 25 years Geordie rowers ensured Tyneside was the centre of the aquatics universe!

*On Screen: Lists of Harry's successes while Narrator talks.*

**ON SCREEN:** "1846 – winners...Manchester Regatta...North of England Regatta...Champion of Scotland."

"1847...winners Durham Regatta ... winners Newcastle and London."

*Posh puppet appears.*

**NARRATOR:** Charles Dickens wrote:

**POSH PUPPET:** The stranger to London aquatics who wishes to see the river at its best should select one of the championship races between professional scullers, especially if London and Newcastle are pitted against each other.

*Posh puppet coughs and disappears.*

**ON SCREEN:** "1848...winners Durham Regatta...

Thames Regatta, winners of the World Championship (*second time*)".

"In 1849 the Claspers rarely lost a race...Thames Regatta - champions of the world (*third time*)."

*Narrator comes stage front.*

**NARRATOR:** By 1849 the Industrial Revolution was in full swing.

While some people lived in luxury, we got a stark reminder of the conditions the vast majority had to endure - a cholera outbreak in Northumberland and Durham took 4,000 lives.

Acute poverty meant TB, congestion of the lungs, was rampant - one-third of all deaths were due to this heinous disease.

**ON SCREEN:** "1850: Victories in Stockton, Durham, Carlisle and Manchester. Harry wins the Tyne Champion belt".

"1852 and 1853 - victories throughout the UK, including Carlisle, Durham and Newcastle".

"1854 - the Henley Regatta - winners of the world title (*fourth time*)."

"1855 - four victories in London and at the Tyne Regatta."

*Narrator comes front stage.*

*No images on screen.*

**NARRATOR:** Between 1846 and 1859, while retaining his world championship seven times, Harry had seven more bairns - an interesting correlation there, don't you think?

By 1859 Harry had been part of a world championship winning team eight times in 14 years.

Some ask, "What was the biggest disappointment in Harry's rowing career?"

He'd have said: "Never winning the individual sculler world championship."

The truth is he never felt good enough to challenge the Thamesmen.

His last individual sculling victory was in 1859, aged 47.

After that he preferred competing in pairs and fours, umpiring and coaching.

*Image of Robert Chambers.*

**NARRATOR:** Robert Chambers was one of Harry's charges. In 1859 Robert became the first Tyne oarsman to win the World Sculling Championship - a title he won four times.

*A baby cries "Waaa, wa."*

**NARRATOR:** Dorothy arrived in February 1860 - making it how many? How many, I've lost count? (*beat*) Oh aye, 12 bairns.

By the year's end Harry's career score was 130 major race

victories in all categories...a record.

He had no more bairns!

Then, on June 5th, 1862, at Balmbra's music hall, Newcastle, *The Blaydon Races* was heard for the very first time at Harry's testimonial.

*Image of Balmbra's and performers.*

**NARRATOR:** Large donations were received from all over the UK and Australia. Harry received the keys to 1 Armstrong Street, Scotswood Road, a public house henceforth to be called The Clasper Hotel - posh, it was...in Cruddas Park.

What? It was posh in them days!

It was also their eighth pub. The first they ever owned.

By 1867, aged 55, and established as a rowing coach and boat builder, after 500 races - more than any other rower - retirement from rowing beckoned.

*Visual: "The 1867 Reform Act enabled one third of adult males to vote."*

**NARRATOR:** A year later, in December 1868, aged 56, owning the Clasper Hotel meant Harry was legally entitled to vote for the first time - he'd been a world champion for 23 years!

By now, with some of the family moving out, the Clasper Hotel was ower big, so Harry moved briefly to the Barley Mow Inn on the Milk Market, off Newcastle Quayside.

In 1869, he took over the Tunnel Inn, at Ouseburn, Newcastle.

*Image of Robert Chambers.*

**NARRATOR:** Robert Chambers ran the King's Head a couple of miles up the road in Pottery Bank, Walker. Tragically, a few months later, Chambers, aged 37, died of TB and 60,000 people turned up for his funeral - a fitting tribute to the greatest natural sculler the world had ever seen.

Then, on July 9, 1870 - Harry had a stroke...some irony there, don't you think?

**SUSANNAH (V/O):** Ladies and gentlemen, it's with great sadness that I have to announce the death of my dear husband.

As you are aware, Harry took ill four days ago.

He passed away, peacefully, in the presence of his family at 10am.

**NARRATOR:** The news spread quickly and was reported worldwide. Grown men shed tears when they heard.

The *Newcastle Chronicle* said...

**SUSANNAH (V/O):** "Harry was the Foster father of the present generation of oarsmen and the father of the modern system of boat racing."

**NARRATOR:** The funeral was held on a Sunday - otherwise it would have resembled a general strike -

130,000 people attended!

The funeral procession was due off from the Tunnel Inn at 2.45pm but people started to assemble hours earlier.

*Death March from Saul plays.*

**NARRATOR:** Leading the funeral was Mr Stephenson's excellent band. The hearse was pulled by four black-plumed horses.

*He steps back.*

**NARRATOR:** Behind the hearse, two hundred local oarsmen and members of the Tyne Rowing Club.

*He steps back.*

**NARRATOR:** Behind these, four mourning coaches containing relatives and close friends.

*He steps back.*

**NARRATOR:** Behind these, friends walking three abreast.

*He steps back.*

**NARRATOR:** Then 18 private carriages containing gentlemen of the neighbourhood.

*He steps back.*

**NARRATOR:** Then, on foot, the general public - Harry's people - thousands of them. Lines of people filled the route, every step of the way.

From Tyne Street along City Road, New Bridge Street, past the Theatre Royal, down Grey Street onto Dean Street and to the river's edge.

Thousands more crammed the bridges. Both banks of the River Tyne were swollen by men, women, boys, girls, babes in arms...whippets.

It took eight hours for the cortege to reach the riverside, a distance of just two miles...Harry's body then traversed the Tyne in a tug appropriately called *The Robert Chambers*.

Hundreds followed on in boats.

Upon reaching Derwenthaugh, over the championship course for the last time, Harry's body was carried to a hearse, over the cinder heaps behind the ovens and chimneys, where Harry was once a coke burner.

Three hours later the procession reached St Mary's churchyard in Whickham.

The church tower was thronged and the grave was reached with difficulty.

The six miles had taken nearly 12 hours to complete...it was two in the morning! By which time, there wasn't a pub with beer left in Whickham.

Harry's statue to this day looks out over his beloved River Tyne.

*An image of James Renforth.*

**NARRATOR:** In 1871, a third tragedy befell Tyne rowing.

James Renforth, aged only 29, who had been inspired by Harry, and who was one of his pall bearers, collapsed while racing in Canada.

TB had stolen another life. Renforth was the World Sculling Champion from 1868 until his tragic death three years later.

He too, was a Geordie hero.

*The image fades. Screen blank.*

**NARRATOR:** But, you see, we're not here to mourn the passing of these pioneers, we're here to celebrate their greatness.

We're here to celebrate working-class virtues - honesty...kindness...humour...determination...self-sacrifice...durability and...solidarity. We're here to celebrate Harry Clasper...we're here to celebrate...Geordie spirit!

*Visual: Words of the Blaydon Races (as seen below).*

**NARRATOR:** (*sings*) "Noo when we gat to Paradise thor wes bonny gam begun; Thor was fower-an-twenty on the 'bus, man, hoo they danced an' sung; They called on me to sing a sang, aa sung them "Paddy Fagan", Aa danced a jig an' swung my twig that day aa went to Blaydon."

*He encourages them to sing.*

**NARRATOR:** Howay!

**ALL:** (*chorus*) "Ah me lads, ye shudda seen us gannin',
We pass'd the foaks alang the road just as they wor stannin';
Thor wis lots o' lads an' lassies there, aal wi' smiling faces,

Gannin' alang the Scotswood Road, to see the Blaydon Races."

*The song finishes.*

*Narrator looks around as we hear poignant (piano) Blaydon Races music.*

*He sits and lights fade.*

*On screen: A picture of Harry's face.*

*A la the opening, industrial noise and cheers. "Hadaway Harry, hadaway lads".*

*Fades.*

*The Blaydon Races tune poignantly plays, slowing until it stops.*

*Harry's picture fades.*

*Light fades.*

*Black out.*

## THE END

# Plays

# THE GREAT JOE WILSON

*A play for four actors/musicians set in three time zones: The present, 1890 and 1841 to 1875.*

*There is a small partition stage back behind which some characters exit (and enter) and get changed.*

*In front of the partition is a table and a couple of stools.*

*There are a couple of chairs stage front, right.*

*Props include: A Joe Wilson (5ft × 4ft) standing placard. It reads "Joe Wilson Night" with an image of Joe Wilson. It is on stage but facing away from the audience. A 6ft (round) copy of the Newcastle City Council Joe Wilson blue plaque. A chest (to store clothing and to put props in). The book Gallowgate Lad. Joe Wilson's Life and Songs by Dave Harker.*

# CHARACTERS

The cast play the following characters:

**Actor 1** (female, age up to 35).

Dawn Jackson (present time) and all other female characters: Aunty Bessie, Ann Wilson, Sissy, Mally Dunn, Bella Wilson and Human Billiard Table (Glasgow).

**Actor 2** (male, age up to 35).

Daryl Jackson (present time), Young Joe Wilson, Joe Wilson.

**Actor 3** (male, age up to 35).

Johnny (present time), Tom Wilson, Ned Corvan, Mr Bagnal, Bella's dad (V/O), Rowley Harrison, John Burnett, Mick Kane, Thomas Fordyce, Glasgow Compere.

**Musician/actor 4** (male, age up to 50).

Phil piano & guitar (present time), Mr Robinson, Mr Allan.

# ACT ONE

*Dawn, Phil and Johnny are on stage as the crowd assembles. They are oblivious to the audience. Daryl (actor 2) is late for what is a pre-show rehearsal for Joe Wilson Night. He is Dawn's brother.*

*Phil, Dawn and Johnny play their instruments intermittently for the next five minutes. This effectively comprises an overture of Joe Wilson songs that we are to hear over the next two hours.*

*During this time, Dawn shows impatience with Daryl's lateness. Dawn wears black boots, jeans, a T-shirt and jacket, over which a Victorian dress can slip quickly to make her look like a Victorian woman.*

*Johnny wears modern black shoes, a collarless shirt and perhaps a waistcoat.*

*Lights down (our show starts).*

**DAWN:** (*on mobile*) Daryl, Daryl.

(*to Johnny, playing guitar*) Johnny, shush, shut up (*he stops playing and puts a large black cloth over the Joe Wilson placard*).

(*on mobile*) What do you mean, "what"? You're ten minutes late for rehearsals, that's what!

Daryl, we have a show in two hours (*she gets cut off*) Daryl! Daryl! Awwwwwwwwww!

*Johnny starts walking off stage.*

**DAWN:** (*to Johnny*) Where are you going?

**JOHNNY:** For a tab.

**DAWN:** What?

**JOHNNY:** (*to audience*) Have you seen what I've got to put up with! You're going to meet a lot of people here tonight (*looks at Dawn*) and some of them are not very nice!

*He exits.*

*Phil leaves piano to walk off.*

**PHIL:** (*to audience*) Ah, don't worry about her, her bark's worse than her bite.

**DAWN:** Where are you going?

**PHIL:** With him.

**DAWN:** Sit down!

*He slinks back to the piano.*

**DAWN:** I don't believe this!

*Unseen, Daryl enters reading "The Gallowgate Lad". He is wearing Victorian clothes, has a beard and carries a backpack containing other items.*

**DAWN:** (*sitting to phone*) Ahhh, Daryl, if you get this message after I've killed you...you were a good brother but you were always a pain in the arse when it came to concentrating on one job. That's why the band broke up, remember!

**DARYL:** What's the problem?

*She jumps.*

**DAWN:** Where have you been? What the hell have you got on your face?

**DARYL:** *(touches facial hair)* Like Joe.

**DAWN:** Look, this is just another one-off gig...we get paid to sing some Joe Wilson songs and then we bugger off asap, OK?

**DARYL:** But Joe Wilson was a proper character, man...look at his photo.

*Dawn briefly looks at the book then her phone.*

**DAWN:** You've now cost us 12 minutes rehearsal time.

Right, we'll start with his most popular song *Keep Your Feet Still Geordie, Hinny,* are you ready? Here we go.

*Phil plays a few chords as Daryl moves off stage.*

**DAWN:** *(to Phil)* Whoa, whoa, whoa. Hang on, hang on.

**DAWN:** *(to Daryl)* Where are you going?

*Daryl drags a chest on stage.*

**DARYL:** I got this dropped off earlier.

**DAWN:** Ready Phil, one, two, three…

> *Phil plays a few chords of "keep your feet still".*

**DAWN:** (*sings*) Keep your feet still Geordie hinny…

**DARYL:** Whoa, whoa.

**DAWN:** What now?

**DARYL:** That wasn't Joe's most popular song and it was actually just called *Keep Yor Feet Still*.

**DAWN:** Yes, well it's one of the few Joe Wilson songs I know.

**DARYL:** Like most people.

> *He gets Joe's Victorian coat and hat out of the chest and hangs them behind the partition while speaking, leaving Dawn frustrated.*

**DARYL:** His most popular songs were likes of *Row Upon the Stairs, Gallowgate Lad*…

**DAWN:** If we can actually get round to rehearsing them, we'll sing them tonight.

**DARYL:** I'm just saying, like.

Geordie anthems like *Keep Yor Feet Still* and *The Blaydon Races* didn't become popular until the 20th century thanks to BBC radio and homesick soldiers in two world wars.

**DAWN:** *(sarcastic)* Fascinating.

**PHIL:** Fascinating!

*She glowers at Phil.*

**DARYL:** I mean, *The Blaydon Races* only became what it was when Newcastle fans sung it after the Second World War.

**DAWN:** And look what good it's done them! *(beat)* Can we just get on, please? *(shouts)* Johnny.

*Daryl takes a batch of lyric sheets from backpack and gives her them.*

**DARYL:** These are the proper lyrics...as written by Joe Wilson. I copied them out of the book. You know, a lot of the lyrics by Joe and Ned Corvan...

**DAWN:** Who?

**DARYL:** Ned Corvan. The very first Geordie professional singer/songwriter. What happened was, right, their radical lyrics were later changed on the sheet music so as not to offend middle class piano players and *(posh)* BBC radio sensibilities.

**DAWN:** It's like a trip down memory lane this.

**PHIL:** *(plays piano and sings)* Granddad, granddad, we love you.

**DAWN/DARYL:** Shut up!

*Phils makes hand gesture.*

*Daryl walks knock-kneed and starts to get changed.*

**DAWN:** Whoa, why are you walking like that?

**DARYL:** To get into character. Joe was knock-kneed...rickets...a lack of vitamins as a bairn.

**DAWN:** Oh, no, no, no. You can stop that right away! We'll have the disability rights people all over us. (*sighs*) Look, we're just here to sing some songs and get paid, OK? Can we start please, or they'll be asking for their money back? (*shouts, frustrated*) Johnny!

*Daryl limps.*

**DAWN:** Stop it!

**DARYL:** All right, all right!

**DARYL:** (*reading the book*) Joe died in poverty, you know? In 1875.

**DAWN:** (*off*) Johnny!

**DARYL:** He was only 33...he was buried in Old Jesmond Cemetery.

**DAWN:** Who?

**DARYL:** Joe!

**DAWN:** Johnny'll be joining him if he doesn't get his backside here soon.

*Dawn takes out phone.*

**DARYL:** An unmarked grave! The bard of Tyneside in an unmarked grave, what do you think of that?

**DAWN:** Not a lot.

**DARYL:** Took him 15 years to get a headstone. His identical twin, Tom, spoke at the unveiling *(imitating Tom, but confident)* as you are aware...

*1890. Lights up on Joe's twin brother, Tom. He's in front of a model of Joe's new headstone (once his first speech is over we can bring the headstone off the stage as the concept has been established). This allows Tom to move about freely to narrate.*

*Tom starts off nervous, perhaps holding his cap and fidgeting (touching hair, going from foot to foot etc) but gets more confident as the story develops.*

**TOM:** *(to audience)* As, um, you're aware, in his brief life wor Joe wrote more than 360 songs and recitations. And he now, well, has a headstone he deserves, thanks to Mr Thomas Allan.

*Lights up on Dawn and Daryl strumming guitar.*

**DARYL:** Thomas Allan of T & G Allan, Joe's music publishers - they later had all the pen shops.

**DAWN:** *(to mobile)* Hello, is that the Samaritans?

**DARYL:** Very funny! Fifteen years to get a headstone! Mind you, Geordie Ridley died in poverty and it took him 140 years to get a headstone - and poor Ned Corvan died...

**DAWN:** Let's guess, in poverty.

**DARYL:** No, in Newcastle (*puts guitar down*). But he was in poverty.

*Daryl moves back stage to exit.*

**DAWN:** I don't beli-

**DARYL:** Poor Ned! His plot's under tarmac in an unmarked grave. (*pops head around partition*) Who'd want to be a 19th century Geordie singing superstar, eh?

*Daryl exits.*

*Lights up on Tom.*

**TOM:** (*to audience*) Joe and me always celebrated wa birthday together. He wrote this for our 17th.

*Joe enters - he's knock-kneed.*

**TOM:** (*clears throat, recites*) Just as mischievous as two bairns can be.

**JOE:** Tommy and Joey fall oot and agree.

**TOM:** Onything pleases or vexes the two.

**JOE:** Owt the one gets, half's th'uther one's due.

**TOM:** Envy and kindness.

**JOE:** A bairn's disposition.

**TOM:** Mischievous an' merry.

**TOM/JOE:** Happy condition.

*They embrace, and Joe exits.*

**TOM:** (*to audience*) Joe was taller than me - I always blame him getting the left tit. Our dad was a cabinet maker - mam was a bonnet maker. We were born in Stowell Street, Newcastle, and as bairns we moved a hundred yards up the road to Gallowgate.

Wa older sister Ann was born in 1834.

Wor John in 1837.

Then our Joe, 20 minutes afore me, on November 29, 1841.

I diven't remember it ower well, though, on account of being too young.

This was the start of the Industrial Revolution...the age of steam...thick smoke belching from the factories and mills...the air cloyed and foul to breathe...men, women and children toiling away in dangerous conditions.

Richard Granger and John Dobson's grand architectural vision transformed Newcastle from a medieval town into a modern city.

Tremendous wealth for the few...acute poverty and chronic overcrowding for the rest.

Disease was rife - from consumption, TB, to cholera.

In 1844 wa dad died...TB. He was only 32. Me and Joe, we were only three and a half.

We had a good mother, though...her constant study bein' for

the good of her bairns.

We attended St Andrew's School in Percy Street.

A bit later wor Joe was nominated to attend St Peters School as a "free scholar".

(*Laughs*) He had to wear green corduroy troosers, a green jacket and a green cap - it was the first time we ever wore owt different - I didn't fancy looking like a pea!

I would say the turning point in Joe's life was probably in 1853.

*Aunty Bessie enters with Young Joe who is wearing a green cap, short trousers and green jacket.*

**AUNTY:** Ahhhh, have you got a girlfriend, Joe?

**YOUNG JOE:** (*coy*) I'm only 12, Aunty Bessie.

**AUNTY:** You'll need to be less bashful if you want to get a lass, mind - hey, and you should start to use a razor an'aal.

Your mam tells iz you're ganna to be a printer when you leave school.

**YOUNG JOE:** Aye, when I'm 14.

**AUNTY:** It's a good trade (*beat*) Wor Tom says you sing in the school choir.

**YOUNG JOE:** Aye.

**AUNTY:** Well, how would you and Tom like to see Ned

Corvan on Saturday?

**YOUNG JOE:** *(excited)* Ned Corvan?

**AUNTY:** Aye. Your Uncle John'll take yous.

**YOUNG JOE:** *(more excited)* Honestly?

**AUNTY:** Yes, man!

*He cuddles her, a bit too strong, choking her.*

**YOUNG JOE:** *(hyper excited)* Cor thanks, Aunty Bessie.

**AUNTY:** Calm doon, pet, you'll give iz a gliff, man.

**YOUNG JOE:** Ned Corvan?! I can't believe it!

*They exit.*

*Applause as Ned Corvan enters from side and sings Bella Gray.*

**NED:** Ladies and gentlemen, calm down, calm down...there's niy fight...now this next song is about a bonny lass called Bella Gray...join in if you knaa the chorus. *(to pianist)* Hit it, maestro please.

*(sings)* "Mony a bonny lass a've seen, but nane aw could adore, like bonny, blithesome Bella Gray - she liv'd doon Fellin' Shore.

An' when aa had maw fustin clathes, aa dress'd mysel' sae gay, an' wi' mony a beatin' heart aw've gyen, to meet maw Bella Gray.

(*chorus*) O Bella Gray, maw bonny Bella Gray! Yer maw delight when Aa stuff maw kite, Me bonny Bella Gray.

The high cut an' the Shuffle tee, she could de them all se fine; Smash, nyen could touch me bonny queen upon the Tyne; Aw gat in such a state wi' luive at neets Aa flogged wor cat, Aw toss'd wor pee-dee owerboard, an' thresh'd me uncle Mat."

*Music stops*

**NED:** (*speaks to audience*) Hey, there's a few dirty minds in here tonight, mind...you should be ashamed of y'selves (*laughs*).

One, two, three.

(*sings*) O Bella Gray, maw bonny Bella Gray! Yer maw delight when Aa stuff maw kite, Me bonny Bella Gray"

(*talks*) I have to warn you, it gets a bit sad now.

One, two, three.

(*sings*) Maw Bella had been at Shields yen day, an' gat wet thro' wi' rain, 'Twas that an' twe black puddins caused poor Bella all her pain

They grip'd her sair - curse a' sic stuff! - the doctors a'things tried, But the puddins they had done the trick, for maw poor Bella died.

*He's upset. He looks at the audience for sympathetic reaction.*

(*speaks*) She was deed, man.

*Audience "ahhh".*

(*to audience*) She was deader than that, man.

*Audience "ahhhhhh"*

(*sings*) O Bella Gray, maw bonny Bella Gray! Yer maw delight when Aa stuff maw kite, Me bonny Bella Gray.

Now ever since that time, d'ye knaw, aw've niver been maysel. Aa've ge'en ower smokin' baccy, and dropp'd off drinkin' yel; Maw clathes winna fit me noo, Aa's like a pick shaft in a poke, For wi' thinkin' on maw Bella Gray, me heart is nearly broke.

*He's upset, crying.*

*Music stops.*

*Audience "ahhhhhh".*

(*speaks to audience*) It was broker than that, man.

*Audience "ahhhhhh".*

(*speaks to audience*) Once more for Bella, eh? One, two, three.

(*sings*) O Bella Gray, maw bonny Bella Gray! Yer maw delight when Aa stuff maw kite, Me bonny Bella Gray

O Bella Gray, maw bonny Bella Gray! Yer maw delight when Aa stuff maw kite...

*Music stops.*

(*speaks to audience*) Big finish, mind, are you coming with iz?

*Audience "yes".*

**NED:** (*speaks*) Howay then.

*Music.*

**NED:** (*sings*) Meeeee bon-ny Bell-a Grayyyyyyy.

**NED:** Thank you.

*Ned bows and exits.*

*Daryl enters singing.*

**DARYL:** (*sings*) Oh Bella Gray, my bonny Bella Gray.

(*speaks*) Inspired by Ned, Joe sang his own songs all around town.

**DAWN:** Are we actually going to do a Joe Wilson song or are we just going to talk all afternoon?

**DARYL:** I'm just saying, Joe's first professional break came on Boxing Day 1864...

*Dawn puts song page in his hand.*

**DAWN:** This one - *The Chep That Knaws Nowt!*

**DARYL:** ...at the 2,000-seat Oxford Music Hall better known as Balmbra's.

*Lights down (Dawn and Daryl exit).*

*Mr Bagnal enters (from side).*

**BAGNAL:** Ladies and gentlemen...thank you, thank you, three months ago we mourned the passing of Geordie Ridley, a tragic loss at only 29 years of age, but tonight I would like to introduce you to this young man who I'm sure will carry on Geordie's fine legacy here at Balmbra's Music Hall...please, a big hand for Mr Joe Wilson.

*Applause as Joe enters (wearing hat and coat) and sings "The Chep That Knaws Nowt".*

**JOE:** Cum lissen awhile tiv a Newcassel ditty, a sang ov experience that's been dearly bowt; te loss this advice sure it wad be a pity, tho it's geen biv a chap that knaws little or nowt.

The reet way te be wise, te knaw nowt pretend, lads, then seun ye'll get knollidge for which uthers hev rowt; They'll tell ye thor secrets, then clivor ye'll fend, lads, for nebody knaws mair than the chep that knaws nowt.

Pretend te knaw nowt, an' ye'll find foaks te tell, lads, advice that you wanted when oppress'd wi' sad thowt; Iv each row ye'll get clear ov an' ugly fell, lads, if ye keep a close mooth an' pretend te knaa nowt.

Foaks think ye knaw nowt, so ne enemy trubbils, they'll oftin speak i' your prisence far mair than they owt; You'll knaa mair nor them that pretend to knaw dubbil, if ye open your ears, an' pretend te knaw nowt

When at justice's bar bad witnesses perjure, be sweerin false oaths inte greet trubbil thor browt, a few eer's transportashun for them is the order, T'wad be better for them te pretend to knaw nowt.

In a corner ye see a lad and lass squeezin, just pass by, an' pretend te be luckin' at owt; if they think that ye see them, it's sure te be teezin, how happy they are when they think ye knaa nowt.

Yor applawse te me sang noo divent refuse lads, te amuse an' instruct ye, i' verses, aw've sowt; if it he sent pleased ye, aw hope ye'll excuse, lads, when ye knaw that its sung biv a chep that knaws nowt.

*Applause, cheering and shouting.*

**VOICES OFF:** More, more!

*Bagnal enters.*

**BAGNAL:** (*to audience*) Calm doon, calm doon. He's already done two encores.

**VOICES OFF:** More, more!

**BAGNAL:** Niy more, I've got to get the place shut by afore midneet.

**VOICES OFF:** More, more.

**BAGNAL:** Gan on then. (*to Joe*) You've got one more song, bonny lad.

*Bagnal silently introduces Joe and exits.*

**JOE:** Thank you. Thank you very much ladies and gentlemen, can I ask you to show your appreciation for my pianist Mr Robinson.

*Applause.*

**JOE:** That's enough appreciation! He'll be asking for more money (*smiles*).

This is something you've all heard at home - a *Row Upon the Stairs*. (*to piano player*). A note please, maestro.

*Piano player plays a note.*

**JOE:** A better one than that!

*Joe sings "Row Upon the Stairs."*

**JOE:** (*chorus*) Oh what tungs i' the row upon the stairs,
Clitterin, clatterin, scandal an' clash,
I' the row upon the stairs

Says Mistress Bell te Mistress Todd,
Ye'd better clean the stairs!
Ye've missed yor turn for monny a week
The neybors a' did theirs!
Says Misteress Todd te Mistress Bell
Aw tell ye Mistress Bell
Ye'd better mind you awn affairs
An' clean the stairs yor-sel
Says Mistress Todd-
When it suits me te think that it's me turn;
Ye've a vast o' cheek te order me, thor's not a wummin born
That keeps a cleaner hoose than me; an' mark ye, Mistress
Bell, ef ye'd oney de the syem as me...ye'd gan an' clean yor-sel!

*Chorus*

Says Mistress Bell- Ye clarty fah,
we was't that stole the beef?
What de ye say? cries Mistress Todd,
"De ye mean that aw'm a thief?"
Let's heh the sixpence that aw lent te treat Meg Smith wi'
gin!
An where's the blanket that ye gat the last time ye lay in?
Says Mistress Bell- Ye knaw yor-sel, the sixpence's lang been
paid,
An' the raggy blanket that ye lent wes ne use then ye said!
A raggy blanket! Mistress Bell cries Mistress Todd - What
cheek!
Yor dorty sockin had two holes, full twice the size last week!

*Chorus*

Says Mistress Todd - Ye greet sk'yet gob
Ye'd bettor had yor jaw
The varry shift upon yor back
Belangs the wife belaw!
Ye lazy wretch! shoots Mistress Bell
Its true thor is ne doot
Last neet ye fuddled wi' Bob the Snob
The time yor man wes oot!

Oh, Mistress Bell! says Mistress Todd,
Ye brazind-luckin slut
Ye may tawk away - te clean the stairs,
aw'll nivor stir a fut!
Afore aw'd lift a skoorin cloot
The mucky stairs te clean,
Aw'd see them turn as black as ye
Ye pawnshop-luckin queen!

*Chorus*

*Applause.*

*Tom enters with a couple of beer bottles and passes one to Joe.*

**TOM:** Three encores, eh?

**JOE:** Aye, I was there till midnight - Bagnall's offered iz a three month residency.

**TOM:** Brilliant! The same place that made Corvan and Ridley superstars!

**JOE:** But turning professional, Tom? What if it doesn't work out? What if I'm not good enough?

**TOM:** Your songs are fantastic, man - this is what all them years playing music rooms was for.

**JOE:** But three months worth of new songs.

**TOM:** Look, Ridley's gone and Corvan's...well, it's no secret Ned's dying...the path's clear for you, Joe.

**JOE:** That's another thing...Ridley didn't have a penny and poor Ned's faring niy better.

**TOM:** You've got your printing to fall back on...or you could become a brushmaker like me...there'll always be demand for brushmakers, you knaa...as long as women clean their stairs, like.

*They laugh.*

**TOM:** Think about it. By printing your own songs, you keep control of your copyright, unlike Corvan and Ridley... that's how they've got no money - that's the most important thing, Joe...keeping hold of your copyright.

And I can sell the song sheets at shows, eh?

**JOE:** (*beat*) Aye, I suppose.

*They shake hands.*

**JOE:** Cheers Tom.

*Ann enters.*

**TOM:** Our Ann's got a spare room upstairs where you can set up your own printing press.

**ANN:** Aye, gan on - but I've a husband and bairn to look after, so I want niy funny business up there.

**TOM/JOE:** What?

**ANN:** I know what you two are like!

*Joe cuddles her.*

**JOE:** Thanks Ann. You're me favourite sister.

**ANN:** Ahhhhh (*realises*) Hey, I'm you're only sister!

*She jocularly lifts her hands to him.*

**ANN:** Stand still while I clash you.

*Joe runs off stage with Ann following him.*

**ANN:** Come here, you're not too big that I can't...

**TOM:** (*to audience, smiling*) So Joe set up above Ann's beer house, The Travellers Rest, at 4 Marlborough Crescent, near Newcastle Central Station.

Joe would write his songs and print his lyrics that we would sell at the shows.

It was exciting times...thousands flocked to see him.

Our Joe was never without a pocket book and pen in his hand...and his heed buried in books.

Around this time I got married...to Ellen Baston...a domestic servant...dom-estic ser-vant, it sounds like one up from slavery!

Our Joe, well he was a bit shy.

He wrote a lot about unrequited love, and some lass called Mally kept getting mentioned in his songs.

*Joe sitting, scribbling in his book.*

**JOE:** (*speaks lyrics*) Aw had te meet young Mally once, Aw'll not forget that neet; she promised tiv us faithfully te be i' Grainger Street.

*Joe stands and sings "Mally Diddent Cum."*

*Music kicks in.*

**JOE:** (*sings*) She wad meet us near the Monument, te me she whisperin' said; but oh! that disappointment. Such misery conveyed.

Aw went roond by the market, but Mally wassent there; Throo Newgate Street an' Blackett Street, Aw wander'd full o care; then went back te the Monument but still aw cuddent see the sweetheart that had promised to meet us faithfully.

Northumberland Street an' Percy Street, aw stagger'd wildly throo, the breezes frae the moor edge cud nivor cool me broo, for fever-heat iv ivry street ne Mally aw cud see; aw went back to the Monument - increasin' misery.

I' Grey Street and i' Grainger Street, for three lang oors or mair, me eyes obscured in grief an' gloom, greet sorrow for me share; At last ah made me way back hyem, but there aw cuddent sleep, for oh! aw nivvor thowt that Mall, her promise waddent keep.

**JOE:** (*sits, writes in book and sings*) Ah had to meet young Mally once.

*Joe keeps looking at books and writing.*

**TOM:** (*to audience*) The *Newcastle Guardian* said: "There is a sensational desire to visit the Oxford Music Hall; it is nightly crowded."

Well our Joe was forever coming up with poetry and bits of lyrics, writing about the people around us...everyday things that happened, you know...overheard conversations.

I remember one day-

*Joe sings "The Landlord's Dowter" (unaccompanied) and physically joshes with Tom.*

**JOE:** (*sings*) Aw's one o' the luckiest lads that's oot, at least that's what they tell us

**TOM:** Joe, man!

**JOE:** (*sings*) An' before aw's deun, thor's nyen 'ill doot the fortin that's befell us

**TOM:** Will you...

> *Tom turns to walk away and Joe pulls him back.*

**TOM:** (*sings*) Aw's efter, aw think, the finest lass that ivor was created.

**TOM:** (*smiles and exits*) Get off, man!

**JOE:** (*sings*) Her fethur - he keeps a pubilic hoose, so nobly she's related.

> *Piano music kicks in. It's rousing.*

**JOE:** (*chorus*) This fine-luckin lass for a queen might pass, An' a queen aw've often thowt her, an' aws the lad if ye want te knaw'd, that's on for the landlord's dowter

Whenivor she gets an order for two for consorts or for theatre, she sends for me an' away we gan, man, she's a real forst-rater; Tho aw knaw she drinks upon the sly, aw waddint say owt tiv her, for the time might cum, an' aw hope it will, when aw can tipple wiv her.

> *Chorus.*

Her fethur he thinks aws up te the mark, an' she thinks thor's nyen truer, an' the aud man says aw'll be landlord there as seun as he turns brewer; at a pawnshop, cheap, the tuther day, the wedding ring aw bowt her; So lads look oot for an open hoose, when aw marry the landlord's dowter.

*Chorus*

*Joe bows and exits to applause.*

**TOM:** (*to audience*) Joe's reputation was spreading like wildfire.

Next he was at Stanley's Tyne Concert Hall, beside Newcastle Central Station - a venue holding 2,800 people.

It had been a whirlwind four months.

Joe needed a calling card.

*Sissy is putting a coat on Joe to have his photo taken.*

**SISSY:** Now, keep still, Joe...and smile. It's not a prison photograph.

**JOE:** How long do I have to...

*Camera flashes.*

**SISSY:** There.

*Sissy helps take Joe's coat off.*

**JOE:** Thank goodness for that.

**SISSY:** So, what s next, Joe?

**JOE:** A month at the Tyne Concert Hall, and then back at

the Oxford. What about you?

**SISSY:** Jack and me we're are off to the fair tonight. See you later, Joe.

*Sissy exits.*

**JOE:** Bye Mally...um, Sissy.

*Joe sings "Mally Dunn".*

*Mally enters.*

**JOE:** Twes at the last October fair, aw first saw Mally Dunn, her bright blue eyes her yallow hair, Me fancy fairly wun; She luckt the queen ov a' the queens that seem'd se happy there, aw wes ower heed an' ears in love wi Mally at the fair.

Says aw, maw canny luckin lass aw'll buy ye owt ye like, Or if sic things ye reckon trash, aw'll tek you for a hike te yon greet shakey shuggy shoo that mykes foaks stop an' stare, Or i' the roondy-boot, nee doot ye'll fettle at the fair

Says she:

**MALLY:** Me lad, that winnet dee, aw think aw've that much sense to knaw when lads myek ower free, Ye'd better keep your pence! Aw've nivor seen yor fyece before - A stranger aw declare shall nivor buy, wi' platry toy, Me fancy at the fair!

**JOE:** Aw liked that little bit conceit, aw's sure it pleased us mair than if she'd craved us for a threat, like uther lasses there, for if, throo bribes, ye win a heart, Yor awn'll seun turn sair, a higher bidder puts ye oot! - aw think it issent fair.

We passed the stalls - aw set her hyem

**MALLY:** Tho' gan away!

**JOE:** She said:

**MALLY:** But if yor shy ye needent try.

Te win a bonny maid!

**JOE:** For time's flew oh - aw've bowt the ring, te marry aw declare.

*Joe goes down on one knee.*

**JOE:** The lass that means to tyek me-sel, tho' she refused me fair!

*Mally exits.*

*Joe downhearted, exits.*

**TOM:** At shows we sold autographed photographs and the printed songs...everyone wanted them.

Then, in May 1865 Ned Corvan died...TB - he was only 37.

Ned was put to rest in an unmarked grave...just like Ridley before him.

But what that meant was, after a mere eight months on the circuit and aged only 23, our Joe was now the undisputed star.

Mind you, I gave it a go mesel, oh aye.

I made me debut at the High Felling Working Men's Institute.

*Piano player exits.*

**TOM:** Hey, where are you going? I sang one of Joe's song's...*Maw Bonny Gyetside Lass.*

*Tom sings unaccompanied.*

**TOM:** Aw warn'd ye hevent's seen me lass - her nyem aw winnet menshun,  For feer ye gan an' tell her hoo aw like her, so aw dee! But it's just for lads an' lasses te whispor thor affecshun, The bonniest lass o' Gyetside's bonny fyece's bother'd me!

The forst time that aw saw her, whey aw's sure aw diddnt knaw her, tho' aw thowt aw'd seen her fyece afore, but cuddint think o' where; Her blue eyes met mine i' passin' up High Street i' the mornin, an' her luck wes si intrancin, that me heart wes mine ne mair!

Aw diddin't see her for a week, till one neet at the Bridge End...when aw stampt upon her goon, an' the gethors com away, she said that aw wes clumsy an aw said that aw wes sorry, an' aw humbly beg'd her pardin - aw wes lickt for what te say.

She said...her muther kept a shop an' sell'd het pies an' candy, an' her bruther wes a cobbler at the high pairt o' the toon; an' she wes a dress-maker - we got se kind tegithor, that aw blist aw'd been se awkword as aw stampt upon her goon.

Aw myed her laff an' slap me lug, wi tawkin lots o' nonsense. But, bliss ye, when you're curtin thor's nowt se gud'll pass; Aw askt her wad y'be me lass an' aw'd tyek y'oot on Sunday, te maw delite, she said aw might, maw bonny Gyetside Lass!

Te maw delite, she said aw might, maw bonny Gyetside Lass!

*Applause.*

**TOM:** Aye, well, the review said I received loud applause... but I knew there was only one Wilson people wanted. Theatre managers queued up to book wor Joe. For the next five years he played every principal venue in the region.

North Shields Theatre Royal - that held 1500.

The Wear Music Hall in Sunderland - now that held 4,000.

Crowds in Darlington and Carlisle flocked to witness a class of entertainment introduced for the first time into these towns.

Bishop Auckland, Joe was there for two months.

Full houses every night.

Then the promoter buggered off with all his money!

He played South Shields, Jarrow, Stanley, Blyth, Middlesbrough, Hartlepool.

Then back to the Tyne Concert Hall in Newcastle.

Times were tough and unemployment rife, but people turned out in their thousands to see our Joe...he entertained them, he educated them...and, for workers, who could lose their jobs at the whim of a boss craving profits, our Joe empathised.

*Daryl, Dawn and Phil stage front sing "Ne Wark" (guitar and tambourine).*

**DARYL:** (*sings*) Ne wark, ne wark.

Aw's weary, aw's wretched, aw wander forlorn, Aw sigh for the neet, an' then wish for the morn; For neet brings ne cumfort, an' morn little mair, I' byeth mind an' body aw's worn oot an' sair.

**ALL:** Ne wark, ne wark.

**DAWN:** Aw wander te places, an' try te get wark
Where "call back agyen" is the foreman's remark;
Thus hopless an' cheerless aw pass mony a day,
Tho the pay-week cums roond - it te me brings ne pay.

**ALL:** Ne work, ne work.

**DAWN:** Thor's nyen can imagine the angwish aw feel
When aw sit doon at hyem to maw poor humble meal
Each bite seems te chowk us, the day seems full lang
An' a that aw de, whey, aw feel tho 'twas rang.

**ALL:** Ne wark, ne wark

**DARYL:** It cannet last always! Aw hope afore lang
wi' wark aw'll be freed frae sad poverty's pang;
For withoot it hyem's dreery, the fire's bright spark turns

gloomy an' dim when at hyem thor's ne wark.

**ALL:** Ne wark, ne wark, ne wark.

*They smile.*

*Phil exits.*

**DARYL:** That works, ironically.

**DAWN:** Yeah, we'll do that one later. It's good, Daryl

**DARYL:** Don't sound so surprised, it's all in here.

*Daryl gives Dawn the book.*

**DARYL:** Joe typified a new kind of music hall that was moving towards respectability, the acts now had to appeal to decent women...prostitutes were giving venues a bad name.

**DAWN:** It wasn't the prostitutes I'd have been worried about, it was the acts!

I mean, look at this (*reads*) one-legged dancers...a shoe-in for an Arts Council grant that one...a unicyclist on the high wire playing the trombone...

**DARYL:** Sounds interesting.

**DAWN:** That, in theatrical parlance, is termed "savage entertainment".

Oh, and what about this...the female "Human Billiard Table" - where did she pot the balls?

*Daryl exiting.*

**DARYL:** People obviously paid to find out, lots of them.

*Dawn exiting.*

**DAWN:** You can imagine theatre managers seeing the pound signs flashing and converting to variety shows.

*Light on Tom.*

**TOM:** In September 1867, the purpose-built, 1100-seat Tyne Theatre and Opera House on Westgate Road, Newcastle opened. Joe played there at the end of the month.

And just like Ned Corvan before him, he would bring the house down.

Joe's lyrics were now being sung everywhere.

*Joe enters.*

*Accompanied by piano, Joe sings the chorus of "Charley's Across the Sea."*

**JOE:** Bonny bright moon, send Charley te me, myek his path leet an' safe on the sea; shine on, ye stars, an' sparkle as free, Charley's across...

Music stops abruptly. Joe remains still as Tom speaks and moves around him.

**TOM:** Then, on May 2, 1868, our sister Ann was taken by TB. She was only 33. (*upset*).

Her son Joseph - who was named after our Joe - died a few weeks later.

A deep change came across wor Joe...a tiredness.

Well, he'd been on the circuit for nearly four years solid.

*Music intro to "Aw Laff Her Bad Temper Away" starts.*

**TOM:** And there was competition.

*Tom puts on white gloves and a bowler hat to become Rowley Harrison.*

**TOM:** Coming up on the inside was Gateshead singer/songwriter Rowley Harrison.

**ROWLEY:** (*sings*) Now, lads Aa'm a new married man, they caal my new wife Fran, Aa de all me best te please her - I do whatever I can.

Oh, they say a wife's one o' yer ribs But Aam'm ganna ask Mistress Gibbs. For if me wife Fran has mair than her aan aa'lll laff her bad temper away.

Aa'lll laff her bad temper awayyyyy.

*Applause.*

**ROWLEY:** (*to audience*) Give over.

*Rowley bows and takes hat and gloves off to become Tom again.*

*Applause dies.*

**TOM:** Rowley was at the Oxford and getting five curtain calls nightly.

Oh, and our Joe, wey, he fell in love, didn't he?

Eh, not with Rowley Harrison, mind.

*Tom exits and Joe enters to applause.*

**JOE:** Thank you. Thank you very much. Now, we've seen some pretty stars on this stage...mind you, not tonight!

But that's about to change with one of the prettiest lasses you've ever seen. Please give hearty applause to Jarrow's very own...Isabella English.

*Bella enters and sings Gallowgate Lad.*

*Joe stands stage side, watches - there is flirtatiousness between Joe and her.*

**BELLA:** "One morn neer the grand Central Stashun
'Mang croods that was hurryin bye
Aw happin'd te see Meggy Bensin
An' sairly the lassie did cry
Says aw-canny lass what's the matter?
Says she, quite dejected. Aw's sad,
Aw's greetin for Jack, that's me luver,
Maw bonny bit Gallowgate Lad!

Ye'll knaw him, Joe, issn't he hansum? (*see looks at Joe*)
As clivor a lad as ye'll see
He works at Stivvisin's Factry
But lately he's been on the spree;
An' he got bag'd for gawn on the fuddle

An' the jewl mun heh fairly gyen mad
When he went an' join'd the Millsha
Maw gud-luckin Gallowgate Lad!

Aw's fairly heart-broke since he left us
Aw cannet leeve weel be me-sel
An' me tung gans as tho 'twad keep tellin
A lang way mair then aw shud tell;
When the heart's full it's greet consolashun
Te whispor what myeks ye se bad
Oh what myed ye join the Milsha
Maw gud-luckin Gallowgate Lad?

Maw gud-luckin Gallowgate Lad.

*Bella is exiting and gets stopped by Joe.*

**JOE:** Excuse me, miss. Th...tha...that's my song!

**BELLA:** I know.

**BELLA'S DAD:** *(off)* Bella!

**JOE:** Bella?

*She nods.*

**JOE:** I know it is, I'm just, eh...is that your husband?

**BELLA'S DAD:** *(off)* Bella!

**BELLA:** *(laughs)* That's me dad!

**BELLA'S DAD:** *(off, angry)* Now!

**BELLA:** (*serious*) I've got to go.

**JOE:** See you soon, eh?

**BELLA:** I hope so.

*Joe grasps her hand and they shake.*

**BELLA:** I have to go.

*Bella giggles and kisses Joe's cheek. She runs off. Joe exits, touching his cheek.*

**TOM:** Well, that was 17-year-old Bella - she was part of the Singing English Sisters. After that, Joe was smitten - always looking to see if they were on the bill. Well, I mean Bella - mind you, she was a bonny looking lass.

*Joe and Bella enter, arm in arm.*

**BELLA:** Hey, Tom...keep August 3, free.

**TOM:** Where are you playing, like?

**BELLA:** I'm not, we're getting married.

**TOM:** That was quick! I mean, great. Where?

**BELLA:** Newcastle Register Office.

**TOM:** Not in church?

**JOE:** No.

**TOM:** I suppose it's cheaper.

**BELLA:** It could be for political reasons, Tom.

**TOM:** Oh, aye. Sorry Bella. Is that why, like?

**BELLA:** No. I'm pregnant!

**TOM:** Congratulations!

*Tom moves in to embrace. Joe thinks it's him but he embraces Bella, leaving Joe on his own.*

**JOE:** Alright, alright, put her down, Tom.

*Tom puts Bella down.*

**JOE:** *(beat)* You know the new music hall being built in South Shields?

**TOM:** The New Alhambra? Why aye.

**JOE:** I've been asked to perform at the opening.

**TOM:** I'd expect that, man.

**BELLA:** And be stage manager.

*Bella kisses Joe and exits.*

**TOM:** *(beat)* Stage manager?

**JOE:** It means no travelling...I'll book the acts and perform ...I'll be in my own bed of a night, Tom.

**TOM:** I'm happy for you Joe, I really am...but this owner...

**JOE:** Mr Siddall.

**TOM:** Aye. He's not going to sell alcohol, man. I mean, music halls rely on alcohol sales! Siddall's a builder...he knows nowt about theatre, he's just chasing the money.

**JOE:** He's asked iz to write a pantomime, one set in South Shields.

**TOM:** A pantomime? But you're music hall, Joe!

**JOE:** It'll get people through the door.

**TOM:** What? That's not your problem, it's Siddall's.

**JOE:** Look, Mr Allan's bought the copyright of the pantomime.

**TOM:** You sold your copyright?

**JOE:** We need the money.

*Joe exits.*

**TOM:** (*to audience*) The pantomime sold well but a music hall with no alcohol meant audiences fell...and within weeks Joe left.

**BABY CRYING:** (*off*) Waaa, waaa!

**TOM:** (*to audience*) On February 6, 1870, Bella gave birth to Joseph junior at 59 Blandford Street, Newcastle...a house Joe and Bella shared with me and Ellen and our brother-in-law John, and obviously their babby, young Joe.

*Joe enters with a 'bairn' (a bundle of rags)*

**TOM:** Of course, Joe wrote a song about it.

*Tom exits.*

*Joe sings Aw Wish Yor Muther Wad Cum. The actions accompanying this song involve Joe with the bairn, sticking it under his arm, sitting on a chair, fumbling, almost dropping the bairn and it wetting his leg (he feels his leg and winces).*

**JOE:** (*sings*) 'Cum, Geordy, haud the bairn
Aw's sure aw'll not stop lang;
Aw'd tyek the jewl me-sel
But really aw's not strang;
Thor's flooer an' coals te get
The hoose-turns thor not deun
So haud the bairn, for fairs,
Ye've often deunt for fun!

Then Geordey held the bairn
But sair agyen his will,
The poor bit thing wes gud,
But Geordey had ne skill;
He haddint its Muther's ways
He sat byeth stiff an' num;
Afore five minutes wes past
He wished its Muther wad cum!

His wife had scarcely gyen
The bairn began te squall
Wi' hikin't up an' doon
He'd let the poor thing fall
It waddent haud its tung
Tho'sum aud teun he'd hum
"Jack and Jill went up the hill"

Aw wish yor Muther wad cum!

Men seldom give a thowt
Te what thor wives indure;
Aw thowt she'd nowt to de
But clean the hoose, aw's sure
Or myek my dinner an' tea
It's startin' te chow its thumb;
The poor thing wants its tit
Aw wish yor Muther wad cum!

What a selfish world this is!
Thor's nowt mair sae than Man;
He laffs at Wummin's toil
And winnet nurse his awn
At last, it's gyen to sleep
Me Wife'll not say aw's num
She'll think aw's a real gud nurse...

*Sounds of baby crying.*

**JOE:** ...Aw wish yor Muther wad cum!

*Joe exits.*

**TOM:** Joe's next move into theatre management came in the same year. (*big gestures*) The Cambridge Music Hall and Theatre Royal...Joe, Bella and Little Joe moved to...Spennymoor.

And I thowt Sunderland was bad! Just joking.

Like Siddall at South Shields, Watson was a builder with an eye for a quick buck. Within two months the family had moved again, this time to Prince's Music Hall in Carlisle.

When Joe wrote this song he must have had Bella in mind (*to pianist*) can we try it in C please, Mr Robinson?

*Music intro plays.*

*Tom exits.*

*Bella enters with a suitcase and sings Miseries O'Shiftin'.*

**BELLA:** (*sings*) I'v a' the troubles that thor is, thor's nyen like weary shiftin, besides the wark it spoils the things, ne matter what you're liftin'.

For Mistress Smith, that leev'd next door, when shiftin to the second floor, alang the street caused sic a stir, the day she started shiftin'.

The next day efter that, she stood, bewilder'd like an' weary, te put things i' thor place she meant wi spirits not se cheery; she luckt aboot, but where te start she diddent knaw, she quite lost heart te try an' myek the hoose luck smart, wes puzzlin efter shiftin.

Her breast wes full o' heavy sighs, the drawers wes full o'scratches. Ses she, "if aw shift ony mair, aw'd like te see them catch us"; The clock weights rowl'd aboot the floor, she hardly knew which way te stir, an' wish'd she'd only knawn before, the misteries of shiftin.

The chair-backs diddent seem te care, for legs that they belang'd te, the luckin' glass wes nicely scraped, the bed wes put up rang tee, for scaircely had they had a snore, when doon they fell upon the floor, an' Jinny cursed, an' Harry swore, the divil tyek the shiftin.

Jinny cursed, an' Harry swore, the divil tyek the shiftin.

*Bella exits to applause.*

**TOM:** Well, Joe went on to manage and perform at the Prince's for 13 weeks.

*Joe enters and composes on seat at table.*

**TOM:** Until July, 1871, when *The Era* newspaper reported that he had the largest benefit concert ever known in Carlisle.

*Bella enters with tea pot and cups, which she puts on the table. Tom stands still.*

**BELLA:** We'll need the money, Joe.

**JOE:** Aye.

**BELLA:** For an extra mouth to feed.

**JOE:** What? Oh, that's great. Come here.

*He cuddles her and flusters over her.*

**JOE:** Sit down pet, sit down...come on.

*He offers her the seat.*

**BELLA:** I'm pregnant, not an invalid, man.

*Tom joins them.*

**TOM:** (*excited*) Congratulations!

*Bella kisses him on the cheek.*

*Tom gives a bar of cholcolate to Bella.*

**TOM:** For the bairn.

**BELLA:** He's about somewhere (*shouts*) Hey Joseph, your Uncle Tom's here.

**TOM:** (*to Bella*) Howay, sit down.

**BELLA:** Don't you start!

**JOE:** So, what's the crack back home, Tom?

**TOM:** Wey, Rowley Harrison's making a big name for himself - you've left a vacuum, Joe. People are wondering when you're coming back. Seven months is a long time, y'knaa.

**JOE:** You haven't come to Carlisle to talk business, Tom. What's happening back in Toon?

*Bella offers a cup of tea in a China cup. He refuses. Joe and Bella drink tea.*

**TOM:** The engineers are on strike.

**BELLA:** Strike? What strike?

**TOM:** 10,000 men out. I mean the lads are working 59 hours a week...many 87 hours just to support their families. It's not right, Joe. The bosses are absolutely coining it in...railways, ships, armaments. And the lads are dying of TB...they reckon a third of them don't even see their 30th birthday.

**BELLA:** When did the strike start?

**TOM:** Back in May. The Sunderland lads came out first and called for solidarity from Tyneside...they got it, an'all...the Wearside employers quickly conceded the 54 hour working week.

**BELLA:** They won?

**TOM:** Why aye...and on Tyneside, Palmer's shipyard and Robert Stephenson's railway works were petrified of a strike...said they'd concede the 54 hours if other employers would.

20,000 people attended a mass meeting on the Town Moor.

It's solid, man, solid. You know, only a quarter of the lads were unionised before the strike?

John Burnett's leading it.

**JOE:** John?

**TOM:** Aye.

**BELLA:** Who's John Burnett?

**JOE:** Wa cousin, on mam's side...he's a good lad, our John.

**TOM:** Aye. Armstrong's bringing in blacklegs from Scotland and Europe. The police are arresting pickets just for looking at scabs.

**JOE:** Armstrong, eh?

**BELLA:** He should have his own guns pointed at his heed.

**JOE:** Aye.

**TOM:** Well, the Wearside lads are sending money over, North Eastern Railway engineers are levying their members and the miners are pledging financial support.

**JOE:** Bella, it's time to pack wa bags.

**BELLA:** I'm not shiftin' again! Niy way!

**JOE:** We're going back to Newcastle.

**BELLA:** About bloody time! (*she grabs cup off Joe as he's about to drink, shouts off, and exits*) Joe...Joe! Howay son, we're gannin y'hem.

*Joe sings The Strike.*

*He's unaccompanied, except with percussion (tea boxes) by the other two male actors.*

**JOE:** (*sings*) Cum, me canny Tynesiders, an lissen
Tiv a sang that aw's sartin ye'll like,
An' aw'll whisper a word kind an' cheerin
Te the mony poor fellows on strike
Let them keep up thor hearts as they hev deun
Thor's a day for the true an' the brave
An' the time 'ill yit cum when greet maisters
Will find oot a mechanic's ne slave!

Is Nine Oors an unreasonable movement?

Is't not plenty for labour te men?
Let them that condemn'd hev a try on't
An' see if they'll alter such plan;
An' if lang oors industry increases,
Heh they fund it wi' them that they've tried?
Wi' thor capital heh they got labour
Like that frae the men they've defied?

But cheer up, thor's gud friends that support us
Aye, an' Ingland depends on us a'
An' we'll prove that wor true te the movement,
An' victory shall let the world knaw
That Tynesiders 'ill nivor be konker'd
Wi' maisters is meant to me maisters,
(*speaks normally*) Let them find thor's men meant to be men!

*Lights out.*

## END OF ACT ONE

# ACT TWO

*Joe and Bella enter from audiotorium. Joe sings The Lads Upon The Wear. Bella, behind Joe, carries a placard that says "Sunderland Supports the Tyneside Strikers".*

**JOE:** (*sings*) What a greet success they've myed
I' myest ivry kind o' trade
Ne shipbuilders I' the world they'll ivor fear
When the Nine Oors Strike begun
It wes gain'd and fairly wun
Forst and foremost, be the lads upon the Wear!

**JOE/BELLA:** (*chorus*) An' ho, me lads, it myeks me heart se glad
Te sing ye a sang te please ye here
Then give a hearty cheer
For the lads upon the Wear
Ay, a hearty cheer for them upon the Wear!

*Applause.*

**JOE:** Thank you, Sunderland. It's my great privilege to introduce you now to the man who is leading the Tyneside engineers' strike, Mr John Burnett.

*Burnett enters to applause.*

**JOHN:** Thank you, thank you. Now, yesterday, the employers offered a 57-hour week but we said no. It's 54 hours - a nine-hour, six day week - or we continue the strike!

*Cheers.*

**JOHN:** Armstrong evicted working people, our people, from their tied houses and gave them to the strike-breakers he hired from Scotland.

*Boos.*

**JOHN:** But, when they discovered they were being used as scabs, the Scots lads went back home...we, the League, even paid their fares!

*Cheers and laughter.*

**JOHN:** The Dutch, Belgian and German workers Armstrong employed, instead of scabbing, went on strike themselves - for the nine-hour working day!

*Cheers.*

**JOHN:** They've gone back to Hamburg, Rotterdam and Brussels to organise workers there. Due to union solidarity, strike pay has gone up from eight shillings to 12 shillings.

*Cheers.*

**JOHN:** We're winning. Thank you Sunderland!

*Cheers.*

*Burnett changes to become Tom.*

**TOM:** Then, on October 9, 1871 - the employers

conceded the 54-hour working week! The strikers did more for the working class than all the bills passed by Gladstone's Liberal Government.

(*aside as exiting*) What's changed?

*Bella enters. She's five months pregnant and sings the chorus of Charlie's Across The Sea.*

**BELLA:** (*sings, unaccompanied*) Bonny bright moon, send Charley te me.

*Joe enters and watches her.*

**BELLA:** (*sings*) Myek his path leet an' safe on the sea. Shine on ye stars and sparkle as free.

*Joe holds her waist from behind.*

**JOE:** You know what, pet?

**BELLA:** What?

**JOE:** I wish I'd never written that song! It's all you ever sing!

*They laugh.*

**BELLA:** But I love it.

*He embraces her.*

**JOE:** And I love...

*Tom enters.*

**TOM:** Happy birthday, Joe.

**JOE:** Happy birthday, Tom.

**TOM:** 30 years old, eh?

*They embrace.*

**TOM:** Mind, Bella you're getting big now, hinny.

**BELLA:** (*smiles*) Only four months to go.

*Tom hands a bar of chocolate to Bella.*

**TOM:** For the bairn.

*Bella exiting.*

**BELLA:** (*shouts off*) Joseph, your Uncle Tom's here.

**JOE:** I'm giving up the touring, Tom.

**TOM:** Seriously?

**JOE:** Aye (*beat*) The new bairn's due in March...and our Joe'll be two in February

We were only three when dad died.

**TOM:** What's brought this on?

**JOE:** He was only two years older than us.

**TOM:** Joe, man!

**JOE:** Look who the Grim Reaper's taken recently...Bob

Chambers and James Renforth both young men, lost to TB, and last year Harry Clasper...three of the greatest rowers ever, all from no more than two miles around here.

**TOM:** Stop being so morbid, man. (*beat*) If it's any consolation, rowers and entertainers are more popular when they're dead.

**JOE:** Well, that's something to look forward to.

*They laugh.*

**JOE:** Seriously, Tom. If owt happens to me I don't want Bella to struggle like our mam did bringing us up.

**TOM:** Hey, man! She'll have the printing press.

**JOE:** I sold that yesterday.

**TOM:** What?

**JOE:** I'm sick of printing.

**TOM:** Joe, man!

*Joe follows Tom to edge of stage.*

**JOE:** Rowley Harrison's taken a pub in Gateshead and he does one-off gigs...

*Tom exits.*

**JOE:** I could do that and write new songs.

*Mr Allan enters.*

**JOE:** It'll only be a loan, Mr Allan...The Royal Adelaide Hotel...on New Bridge Street.

**ALLAN:** A pub?

**JOE:** Aye, the licence is up for sale - I'll pay you back.

**ALLAN:** But I'm teetotal, Joe.

**JOE:** When did principles ever get in the way of men making a profit, eh? They tell me Armstrong's a pacifist!

Come on, Mr Allan...I've got friends and supporters who'd come along...Ned Corvan did it in South Shields.

**ALLAN:** Aye, but Ned only lasted three years.

**JOE:** But I'll make a go of this, and you know I'm a man of my word.

**ALLAN:** True.

*They shake hands and Mr Allan exits.*

*Bella, heavily pregnant and tying a pinny, enters.*

**TOM:** Ladies and gentlemen, welcome to The Royal Adelaide Hotel.

*Bella and Joe pull imaginary pints.*

**JOE:** (*to imaginary friends*) Hello Matty...Alan. Are you all right Bobby? Haven't seen you lads since the strike.

**TOM:** Hello Jack, good to see you, man.

**BELLA:** What fettle Peggy? (*to Joe*) She's worse than a hangover that one.

**JOE:** Aye, I'll have a gill, Billy...no, a gill'll do.

No, ne whisky, Tommy, just a gill...I've had a couple of pints tonight...you've got hollow legs, ye...aye, I love you too, Tommy.

**BELLA:** Hey, howay, Ernie, there's niy call for language like that.

**JOE:** (*to lad*) Just call iz Joe, son, not Mr Wilson...you saw iz where? The Tyne Theatre? Oh, aye, I like it there...and the Oxford?

**BELLA:** Hey, do you want to hear a new song? Aye?

Howay, Tom.

*Bella drags Tom on and the three sing The Row iv a Public Hoose.*

**JOE:** When a man gets drunk, aw've heard it said, he's sure te speak his mind.

**BELLA:** An' seldum knas when he commits owt oot the common kind.

**JOE:** O' beerhoose crack.

**BELLA:** Or drunken chaff

**JOE/BELLA:** But if ye'll list to me, aw'll let ye hear the row between two spunges on the spree.

**TOM:** An 'aw'll tell ye hoo the row begun, wi splitterin, splutterin, stutterin and ivry kind of abuse, I' that awful row, ridiculous row, the row iv a public hoose!

Says Dick:

**BELLA:** Aw's better like then ye, yor heed's as thick as stone!

**TOM:** Says Jim:

**JOE:** Thor's sumthin i'me heed, yors a' lies i' the bone. Aw'd better hev a heed se thick, te haud what it contains, than heva boiler pyet like yors, that nivir held ne brains!

**TOM:** Says Dick:

**BELLA:** Ye cannet work like me, aw've thorty-bob a week, aw cud lay the factory in me-sel!

**TOM:** Says Jim:

**JOE:** Ye bubly sneak. If ye can myek yor thorty-bob, what myeks ye cadge o'me? Ye askt un in te hev a gill, an' myed us pay for ye!

**TOM:** Says Dick:

**BELLA:** Aw diddent ask ye in, ye cum wi me yor-sel, aw nivor said aw'd pay for ye, aw only pull'd the bell!

**TOM:** Says Jim:

**JOE:** Yor like yor shabby wife, thors nyen as knaw se mean, ye weel may button up yor coat, yor shirt's not ower clean!

**TOM:** An 'aw'll tell ye hoo the row begun, wi splitterin, splutterin, stutterin and ivry kind of abuse, I' that awful row, ridiculous row, the row iv a public hoose!

Says Dick:

**BELLA:** Ye'd better mind yor-sel or else aw'll smash yor nose!

**TOM:** Says Jim:

**JOE:** Oh it's a fight ye want? Aw'll gi ye such a doze. Ye'll nivir want anuther mair, aw'll myek ye black an' blue, aw re'd the Sportin Life last week, an copt a point or two!

**TOM:** Says Dick:

**BELLA:** Aw divvent want te fight, tho ye insulted me!

**TOM:** Says Jim:

**JOE:** Was't me that challins'd ye? Aw'll tell ye what we'll de, we'll let wor fam'ly 'fairs alyen, aw'll riccomend a plan, the way to hev a quiet spree...

**JOE/BELLA:** ...let's byeth pay for wor awn!"

*Bella clasps stomach.*

**BELLA:** Wor Thomas is knocking on the door, pet.

**JOE:** Bella!

*Joe and Tom fluster as they lead Bella off stage "you're all right".*

**BELLA:** Ahhhhhhhh!

*Bella exits with Tom.*

*Joe sings Wor Canny Second Born.*

**JOE:** Just two eers since a lad was born, te mek glad wor fireside, it fills its muther an' me-sel wi nowt but honest pride; we thowt ov a' bairns i' the world, him bonniest an' the best, an thowt we cud luv nyen as much, but noo we've had the test.

*(chorus)* Wor second-born's as big a pet, we mun give him a turn, he's cum te share the forst one's luv, wor canny second-born.

*Bella (not pregnant) enters and sings.*

**JOE/BELLA:** His bonny cheek like velvet soft, wes press'd wi gentle care, the little fellow seem'd te knaw 'twes reet te hev his share; carresses an' the sweetest words, myest ivrything we've tried, we've kiss'd him when we've seen him smile, an kiss'd him when he's cried.

**JOE/BELLA:** *(chorus)* Wor second-born's as big a pet, we mun give him a turn, he's cum te share the forst one's luv, wor canny second-born.

**JOE/BELLA:** He's cum te share the forst one's luv, wor canny second-born

*Joe and Bella embrace and kiss. Bella exits. Joe sits, pensive. Tom enters with two beer bottles.*

**JOE:** *(startled)* Ahhhh. Tom, man.

**TOM:** Time for a spree, bonny lad

*Joe's unresponsive.*

**TOM:** What's wrong?

**JOE:** I'm worried, Tom.

**TOM:** Let's guess, death's ghostly fingers are lurking again!

**JOE:** Aye, but not for me, wey, I hope not. It's just...

**TOM:** What, man?

**JOE:** Wey, the Poor Law Union reckon a quarter of Newcastle bairns die in infancy.

**TOM:** Look, Joe. Joseph's fit and strong...and Thomas...he's three months old now.

**JOE:** Aye, but look what's waiting around the corner... smallpox, scarlet fever, diphtheria, whooping cough, diarrhoea, cholera, TB.

Physical violence.

**TOM:** Joe, if you intend to drive a man to drink you're doing a canny job of it!

**JOE:** It's this place as well...it's gettin iz down, man...the drunkenness, the violence, the bad language.

**TOM:** And that's just you!

**JOE:** It's not funny, Tom...there's men spending money that should be going to keep their wife and bairns.

*Tom offers a bottle, Joe declines.*

**JOE:** Sorry, Tom, I'm not good company tonight.

**TOM:** That's all right, man. Nowt's a bother. I'll see you later, eh?

**JOE:** Aye.

*Tom exits, touching Joe on shoulder.*

**JOE:** Howay, sup up - I've got two bairns to see to.

(*ushering an invisible Jack out*) I'll have a drink with you at the weekend, eh, Jack? Aye, I promise...howay, your lass'll be waiting up for you...you've got work tomorrow.

(*shouts*) Waak n' taak, lads. Howay.

*Bella enters.*

**BELLA:** Time to gan y'hem lads and lasses.

*A drunken, aggressive Mick Kane staggers in.*

**KANE:** How, wench, giz a whisky.

**JOE:** We're closed - and I barred you a month ago.

**KANE:** (*to Bella*) How ye...I'm talking to you...

*Kane grabs Bella's arm.*

*Joe restrains Kane from behind and leads him off stage.*

**BELLA:** Gan canny, Joe.

**KANE:** (*mocks*) Gan canny, Joe. Ha, it's easy to see who wears the troosers in this hoose.

**JOE:** You should be ashamed of yourself, Mick Kane.

*Joe lets go of Kane, who swings at Joe but misses. Joe grabs him.*

**KANE:** I'll have ye Wilson, and her.

*Joe throws Kane off stage.*

**JOE:** And never come back!

*Piano intro as Bella and Joe sing Hannah's Black Eye.*

**JOE:** (*chorus*) Hannah's got her eye blackt, but hoo it wes deun.

**BELLA:** (*chorus*) Aw knaw little mair than the man i' the meun.

**JOE:** (*chorus*)) It might been for fairs or it might been for fun.

**BELLA:** (*chorus*) But it spoils her gud lucks ne matter hoo deun!

**JOE:** She said twes a bed-post she struck i' the dark
Then said it wes deun throo a little bit lark
Wi' Peggy the mangil wife doon i' the lane
But Peggy said diffrint, an' hinted "Mick Kane".

**BELLA:** Ye'll a' understand that Mick Kane is in fact

He rarely gets wark and he seun gets the sack;
He's lazy, he's thievish, an' ivrything bad
An' still Hanna's teun the big loon for her lad!

**JOE/BELLA:** Hannah's got her eye blackt, but hoo it wes deun
Aw knaw little mair than the man i' the meun;
It might been for fairs or it might been for fun
But it spoils her gud lucks ne matther hoo deun!

**JOE:** Aw's sartin it's him that's disfigor'd her eye
An' silly-like she te conceal him 'ill try;
The bonny bright eye that once dazzled the views
As black as her life 'ill be a' the way throo.

**BELLA:** Aw mean if she marries the good-for-nowt cull
She'll sup bitter draughts frev a cup ower full;
For if before marridge te strike her's his plan,
What will he de tiv her shud he be her man?

**JOE/BELLA:** Hannah's got her eye blackt, but hoo it wes deun
Aw knaw little mair than the man i' the meun;
It might been for fairs or it might been for fun
But it spoils her gud lucks ne matther hoo deun!
Hannah's got her eye black't!

*Bella exits.*

*Tom enters and hands a couple of bars of chocolate to Joe.*

**TOM:** Here.

**JOE:** Thanks, Tom.

**TOM:** For the bairns!

**JOE:** Oh! Bella's bathing wor Thomas (*shouts off*) Joseph, Uncle Tom's here.

**TOM:** Well, happy birthday, bonny lad.

**JOE:** Aye, we're 31 today.

**TOM:** You're supposed to smile.

**JOE:** Oh, Tom, man. What have I done?

**TOM:** What's the matter?

**JOE:** If I drink with everybody that asks iz, I'm a drunken beast and if I divent, I'm a surly beast. Apart from wor Thomas being born, 1872 'll go down as the worst year of my life. I have to be oot o' here, Tom, away from this pub, and the drunkards. Did you hear about the murder in Toon last night?

**TOM:** Aye, apparently they've got someone for it.

*They exit.*

*Dawn, with the book, recites Murder Throo Drink.*

**DAWN:** They've teun him off te the station noo, sumbody said that they always knew, 'T'wad end like this; for the fearful strife wad only end i' the loss of a life, an' that wad be i' the life ov the wife.

"Murder!" wes whispered in ev'ry breeth, a poor aud wummin wes kicked to deeth - aye, kicked to deeth wiv her man's greet feet, in hob-nail beuts, that he wore in the street, an sumbody said...that it sarved her reet.

Oh, but sumbody here shud stop an' think, ov the evil deun throo the evil drink. For it's murder here and it's murder there, it's murder throo drink myest iverywhere...an' the gallows is varry seldom bare.

(*beat*) Well, we'll not be doing that one tonight!

*Lights up on Joe, Mr Allan and Tom (playing tambourine) who clap and sing Teetotal Noo.*

**ALL:** (*chorus*) Teetotal noo! Teetotal noo! It cheers the heart a' throo, an' he's teetotal noo.

**JOE:** (*speaks*) Come on, Mr Allan, get them singing.

*They encourage the audience.*

**ALL:** (*sings*) Teetotal noo! Teetotal noo! it cheers the heart a' throo, an' he's teetotal noo.

*Mr Allen hands out leaflets as Tom plays tambourine.*

**JOE:** (*sings*) Ive a' the cures that's in the world, thor's one that's stud the test, an seun 'ill be established as the safest an' the best; that's abstinence frae alcohol, it cheers the heart a' throo...te hear anuthur member's myed...and he's teetotal noo

**ALL:** Teetotal noo, teetotal noo, it cheers the heart a' throo, and he's teeeeeee-total nooooooooooo.

*Tom exits.*

**ALLAN:** (*to audience*) Thank you everyone, thank you for coming. (*to Joe*) I'm sorry the Adelaide never worked out, Joe. I'm glad you signed the pledge, though.

**JOE:** I can't speak for others, but some of the things I saw...Anyway, I'd like to pay some of my debts. I was wondering if you would take copyright of some songs in lieu of payment?

**ALLAN:** Copyright? Are you sure?

**JOE:** (*angryish*) I said I'd pay you back! (*beat*) Sorry.

**ALLAN:** But how will you provide?

**JOE:** Mr Fordyce has offered iz a job as a printer, compositing.

**ALLAN:** Fordyce?

**JOE:** Aye, on Dean Street - I'll work for him and take what shows I can.

*They shake hands, Allan exits.*

**TOM:** (*to audience*) In January, 1873, Joe performed at the Oxford - his last in Newcastle for 16 months. Always popular in Sunderland, he sometimes teamed up with (*puts on white gloves and bowler hat*) Rowley Harrison. They'd play the Wear Music Hall in Sunderland and bring the house down.

*Joe and Rowley sing Dinnet Clash the Door!*

**JOE:** Oh, dinnet clash the door! aw've tell'd ye that before Can ye not let yor muther hev a rest? Ye knaw she's turnin

aud, an' for eers she's been se bad
That she cannet bear such noises i' the least.

**BOTH:** (*chorus*) Then oh, lass, dinnet clash the door se
Yor yung an' yor as thowtless as can be
But yor muther's turning aud
An' ye knaw she's varry bad
An' she dissent like to hear ye clash the door.

**ROWLEY:** She once wes yung an' strang, but bad health 'ill put foaks rang, An' she cannet bear the noise that once she cud; She's narvis as can be, an' whativor else ye de, Ye shud study what ye think 'ill de her gud!

**BOTH:** (*chorus*) Then oh, lass, dinnet clash the door se
Yor yung an' yor as thowtless as can be
But yor muther's turning aud
An' ye knaw she's varry bad
An' she dissent like to hear ye clash the door

**ROWLEY:** (*exiting*) Thank you, thank you - we're here all week.

*Applause.*

*Joe sits to write.*

*Fordyce (with glasses and hat on) enters with a pile of manuscripts in a briefcase.*

**FORDYCE:** Joe

**JOE:** Mr Fordyce?

**FORDYCE:** I've got a job here...for Mr Allan...I have to

tell you it's a bit sensitive, though

**JOE:** What is it?

**FORDYCE:** Typesetting these.

*Fordyce brings out a few manuscripts and Joe takes them.*

**JOE:** (*he reads*) *The Chep That Knaws Nowt...Gallowgate Lad*

**FORDYCE:** I can fully understand if you don't want …

**JOE:** (*he reads*) *Miseries of Shiftin...Row Upon the Stairs* ... these are all mine.

**FORDYCE:** Were...um, were, Joe - apparently you sold the copyright to Mr Allan.

**JOE:** There must be a hundred of my songs here.

**FORDYCE:** Nearly 200, actually.

**JOE:** And look, there's marks through some of the words...he's changed my lyrics.

**FORDYCE:** Yes, well, they're his songs now. I'm sorry Joe.

*Fordyce takes lyrics, puts them back in the briefcase with glasses and hat and becomes Tom as Joe exits.*

**TOM:** The book sold well. As did the songs by Ned Corvan, Geordie Ridley and other Geordie songwriters who also sold their copyright to Mr Allan.

*Lights up on Dawn, reading the book as Daryl enters with a guitar.*

**DAWN:** It says here Thomas Allan made 200 per cent profit on the books.

**DARYL:** He let Joe sell the books at gigs...he got a 25 per cent discount!

**DAWN:** That's...that's just theft.

**DARYL:** Legal theft! It's okay to rob people, apparently - if it's done by a businessman.

**DAWN:** Aye.

**DARYL:** The upshot was, Allan moved to a mansion in Jesmond and Joe ended up in a damp slum in Railway Street, behind the Central Station.

**DAWN:** That's a disgrace.

**DARYL:** Joe must have known what it was like to be skint. He wrote this one, called *Charity*.

*Daryl puts down guitar and recites charity.*

**DARYL:** A poor aud wife, iv a lonely room,
Sits biv hor-sel i' the darknin gloom;
I' the grate thor's just the faintest spark
Te frighten away the dreary dark,
There she sits till she totters te bed,
An'mony a day this life she's led;
Withoot a frind te cum near te speak
She's starvin on fifteen-pence a week.

The parish allows her half-a-croon!
Half-a-croon i' this florishin toon!

Fifteen-pence she pays for the rent
Hoo is the fifteen left to be spent?

Wi' prayer she welcum's the mornin's leet;
Welcums the leet, tho' it brings ne meat;
Welcums the leet o' the mornin gray,
Te sit biv hor-sel the lang weary day
Tho' wishin her awn poor life away,
She clings tid still while she hes te stay.

For, oh, she knaws that she dissent disarve
Te finish her days like this - te starve!
An' ninety eers, if she leeves to see;
In a few short munths her age 'll be;
Withoot a frind i' the world te say-
Canny aud wife, hoo are ye the day?

Can ye compare this case to yor-sel?
An' bring te mind that aw cannet tell,
Yor daily wants that ye daily seek,
Supplied on the fifteen-pence a week.
Is this not eneuff to myek ye fear
Yor-sel an' bairns when yor end draws near?

*Lights up on Tom.*

**TOM:** By 1873, Joe'd been on the circuit for nine years. It's a long time. His early fans had moved on...had families...died. And having had a year off to run the Adelaide, Joe was starting from scratch. He was selling his new songs to Mr Allan - and still performing live.

His greatest hits.

People in concert halls didn't want to hear teetotal songs.

*Joe enters.*

**JOE:** (*sings*) 32 today, 32 today. Happy birthday, Tom.

**TOM:** Happy birthday, Joe.

*They embrace.*

**TOM:** Owt happening?

**JOE:** Aye a gig next week, in Consett, and I got this photograph taken.

*Joe shows him a photo of himself.*

**TOM:** Smart.

**JOE:** It's for when music hall proprietors say "Joe Wilson? That name's familiar. Oh, aye, I remember. let's book him."

*Joe coughs.*

**TOM:** You'll need to get that cough seen to, mind.

**JOE:** You sound like Bella.

*Bella enters with newspaper.*

**TOM:** Oh, hello, pet.

**BELLA:** Tom.

*They cuddle.*

*Joe coughs.*

**BELLA:** Can you have a word with him to get that cough seen to?

**JOE:** Here we go again! (*coughs*).

**BELLA:** It's bad news.

**JOE:** I haven't been diagnosed yet, Tom, and she's-

**BELLA:** No, the general election! The Conservatives have won 52 more seats than the Liberals.

*She hands Joe the paper.*

**JOE:** Their first victory since 1841.

**BELLA:** 33 years.

**TOM:** I can't believe it.

**JOE:** What happened to the militancy of a few years ago?

**TOM:** Looks like skilled workers have more money in their pockets - and they've pulled the bloody ladder up.

**JOE:** But workers voting Conservative, Tom! Are they stupid?

**TOM:** Some are, obviously - those with property rights to vote - but there's no proper choice, the Liberals are just Tories in disguise...we need a party of labour, Joe.

**JOE:** Aye. One day, Tom, one day.

**BELLA:** Do you want some good news, pet?

**JOE:** We could do with some.

**BELLA:** I'm pregnant.

**JOE/TOM:** What?

**BELLA:** Three months.

**JOE:** I don't believe it! Brilliant! How did that happen?

**BELLA:** The same way as the other two!

*They laugh. Joe has a coughing fit.*

*Joe and Bella exit.*

**TOM:** (*to audience*) In the spring of 1874 Joe toured further afield. The New Gaiety Theatre, West Hartlepool. The Oxford Music Hall, Middlesbrough. The Theatre of Varieties in Brotton, North Yorkshire. The Wear, Sunderland. Full houses and storms of applause greeted him. He was much in demand, not only in northern England, but in Scotland. In May, 1874, he performed at the world-renowned Britannia Music Hall in Glasgow.

*Joe enters. He's nervous.*

*Tom becomes a Scottish compere, wearing an eye patch.*

**COMPERE:** Hey, Geordie, welcome te Glasgae. I'm the compere...you nervous?

**JOE:** Just a bit.

**COMPERE:** Do you want my advice?

**JOE:** Aye.

**COMPERE:** Just forget that this audience for generations sought entertainment from public flogging and hanging. (*laughs*).

**JOE:** Thanks!

**COMPERE:** Och, dinnae worry, man. Dinnae worry. If they dinnae like'ye, you'll soon know.

*We hear loud booing as the pianist drags a body from behind the partition.*

**COMPERE:** Och, they dinnae like human billiard tables here. Get on the noo, go on, - or there'll be a riot!

*The compere drags the body off.*

*Musician returns to piano.*

**JOE:** (*sings*) Aud Mistress Clark wes fond o' clash, she lik'd te hear her tung, she said that tawkin eased the mind, wi foaks byeth aud 'n young.

The chep that knaws nowt's gud advice wes lost on Mistress Clark, but mind aw shuddint mentshun this, aw hope ye'll a' keep it dark.

Says Mistress Clark te siv'ral frinds, she had one te tea, aw wunder what myeks Geordy Hall se fond o' beer an' spree?

They say his wife can tyek her gill, an neether's fond o' wark, but mind aw shuddint menshun this, aw hope ye'll a' keep't dark!

There's Dolly Green, that dorty slut, that leeves alang the yard, she flirts wi' every lad she meets, she's worthy ne regard, last neet I catch'd her on the stairs wi Jack the Keyside clerk; But mind, aw shuddint menshun this, aw hope ye'll keep't dark.

But mind, I shuddint menshum this, aw hope ye'll a' keep it dark.

*There's loud applause.*

**JOE:** Thank you, thank you.

Now, eh, I'm a happily married man...don't sound so disappointed, ladies, but this next song is about being young...and shy.

*Joe sings Bonny Sally Wheatley.*

**JOE:** Noo Aw's byeth diprest an' sad, tho' aw once wes blithe an' glad an' cud trip aboot the toon byeth trim an' leetly.

Aw wes happy neet and morn, But iv aw sic joys Aw's shorn, since aw fell se deep i' luv wi' Sally Wheatley.

(*chorus*) O dear me, aw dinnet knaw what to de, for Sally's teun me heart away completely, an' aw'll nivor get it back, for she gans wi' Mistor Black, an' they say he' gan te marry Sally Wheatley.

Hoo aw felt aw dinnet knaw, the first time aw Sally saw, in a threesum-reel she hopt aboot se leetly; An' aw might hev had a chance if aw'd askt her up te dance but aw wes ower shy to speak to Sally Wheatley.

*chorus*

So, as often is the case, ye'll fin'd uthers i' yor place if ye dinnet shuv ahead - an' fettle reetly, for aw'd scarcely turn'd me back when aw there saw Mistor Black - he wes jiggin' roond tha room wi' Sally Wheatly.

*chorus*

An' he mun hev myed it reet, when he set her hyem that neet - efter work, drest up, he gans te see hor neetly; thor's greet danger i' delay, or aw'd not been sad the day: if aw had a heart aw'd brick't for Sally Wheatley.

*chorus*

*As applause dies, Joe clutches his side. Compere enters, hurridly.*

**JOE:** Ahhhhhhhh!

**COMPERE:** Are you alright there, Geordie?

**JOE:** Ahhh, a pain in my side - like a knife!

**COMPERE:** A knife? I wouldnae put it past this rabble. (*points at audience*) Which one of you lot's throwing knives? (*points*) You?

**JOE:** No, like a knife...I'll be alright.

*Joe staggers to chair, coughing.*

*Compere becomes Tom (takes off eye patch).*

**TOM:** Joe came home and continued to sing at The Oxford but doctors ordered him to take a rest.

*Bella, looking six months pregnant, enters with sheets of paper.*

**BELLA:** Mr Allan's here. Here. (*gives Joe the sheets of paper*).

**JOE:** Thanks, pet.

**BELLA:** You shouldn't be working.

**JOE:** What am I supposed to do, just sit here all day?

**BELLA:** You're supposed to be resting.

**JOE:** I'll be alright.

*Joe stands up and coughs.*

**BELLA:** I give up!

*Mr Allan enters.*

**BELLA:** (*nods*) Mr Allan (*to Joe*) No exertions!

**JOE:** Alright, man, woman, man.

*Bella exits.*

**JOE:** She's making iz sound worse than I am.

*Joe gives sheets of paper to Allan.*

**JOE:** (*coughs*) There's 20 temperance songs here.

*Allan gives him some money.*

**ALLAN:** Money for copyright...and that, um, loan we talked about.

**JOE:** I've written out an IOU...for £17.10.

*Allan takes the IOU.*

**JOE:** Not a word to Bella, mind.

*Joe exits.*

*Allan becomes Tom.*

**TOM:** Mr Allan published a book called *Joe Wilson's Temperance Songs*. About 60 songs. Like the last, it was very popular and sold well.

*We hear a baby noise.*

**TOM:** Then, on July 25, 1874, Robert John Wilson was born at 47 Railway Street, Newcastle.

*Joe enters, holding a baby and coughs intermittently.*

**JOE:** Born two hundred yards from the Tyne, Robert. You're a proper Geordie. The son of a great city where we aal taak propa. What a world you've been born into. The age of steam and gas lighting. When I was a lad we had candlelight...mind you, in an age of magnificent scientific discovery, you might well ask why we live in a damp house.

*Sound of a steam engine.*

**JOE:** Hear that, son? That's a steam engine, opposite...in the Central Station.

*He becomes very emotional.*

**JOE:** When you get older I'm going to show you all the things I got up to with your Uncle Tom when we were bairns, around here...before the Central Station was built...when it was just fields...and when we saw Ned Corvan.

*Bella enters and comforts him.*

**JOE:** I'm sorry, pet.

**BELLA:** What for?

**JOE:** (*he hands Robert to Bella*) Take the bairns away from here.

**BELLA:** Why?

**JOE:** When I'm gone. The air's better in Northumberland, or Durham.

*They embrace, tearfully.*

*Bella exits with young Robert.*

**TOM:** Joe soldiered on throughout the summer of 1874, despite his illness.

*Joe coughs and looks at blood on his handkerchief; he's visibly declining in health and strength as Tom speaks.*

**TOM:** Two weeks at the Victoria Music Hall, Newcastle. Six nights at The Wear, Sunderland. Dates at the Oxford, Middlesbrough. He made his last ever public performance on September 4, 1874, at the Royal Star Theatre of Varieties in Stockton.

And for your headlining act tonight, it gives me a great honour to present...

The one, the only...Mr Joe Wilson

*Applause.*

*Joe's very ill, coughing. A quivering voice, It's a painful performance. Joe sings The Time That Me Fethur Wes Bad.*

**JOE:** Thor wes greef i' the hoose all aroond
An' the neybors luckt in passin by
An they'd whisper "Hoo is he the day?"
Then hing doon their heeds wiv a sigh
An they's speak te me muther se kind
tho whativer they said myed her sad
an she'd moan real heart-broke tiv her-sel
A' the time that me fethur wes bad
As me fethur lay ill iv his bed as helpless as helpless can be
Man it myed me heart ache when he tried
te smile at wor Johnny an me
For he wes always fond ov his bairns
An aw mind Johnny said..."get up, dad!" (*upset, coughs uncontrolably*).

*Bella enters (carrying a case) and holds Joe.*

*They are joined by Rowley Harrison (perhaps wearing white gloves).*

**ROWLEY:** How are you doing, Joe? Howay in, bonny lad. Get yourself sat down. Howay, man. No rush, no rush.

*Rowley guides him to a stool. Joe sits.*

**ROWLEY:** (*sees case*) I'm sorry Bella.

*Rowley takes case off Bella.*

**BELLA:** Thanks Rowley.

**ROWLEY:** Welcome to our humble abode, the Commercial Hotel. Joe can stay as long as he wants, so don't worry - the air up here in Winlaton is fresher than in Toon...we'll have him better in no time, eh, Joe?

**JOE:** Aye.

**ROWLEY:** I'll take this [*case*] up.

*Rowley exits.*

**BELLA:** I'll bring the bairns up on Sunday. If you want to come home any time, Joe, I'll be straight here to collect you.

*She holds and kisses his hand as she sings (unaccompanied) Charley's Across The Sea.*

**BELLA:**  Bonny bright moon, send Charley te me
Myek his path leet an' safe on the sea;
Shine on, ye stars, an' sparkle as free (*too upset to finish*).

**JOE:** (*struggling to sing*) Charley's across the sea.

*Bella exits, upset.*

*Joe holds a letter (he later reads from it).*

*Tom enters with a yellowing letter.*

**TOM:** Dear Tom. The Adelaide debt is now paid off. The other good news is Mr Allan organised a benefit at the Mechanics' Institute. The money will see the family through the winter. The only thing I desire now is to see my children reared.

**JOE:** And I've got a great idea - *"Joe Wilson's Comic Tyneside Almanac"*.

**TOM:** Laffable songs, comic stories, queer drolleries etc.

**JOE:** What do you think, Tom?

**TOM:** I've been at Rowley's for a month now. I'm coming home for our birthday on the 29th.

**JOE:** Only death'll stop me from celebrating that with you, dear brother. I thought you might like this. I wrote it this morn...*(recites)* Good luck to 18 sivinty five

**TOM:** May we all be contented and thrive, an wi lucky cuts contrive...te keep health and strength alive. Myek wor hyems a bissy hive, as honestly we strive

*Joe drops the letter and slumps over.*

**TOM:** An' may ne bad luck deprive us ov owt we'd hev arrive...an throo care an trouble drive

I' the year o'sivinty five

(*to audience*) On Sunday, February 12, 1875, our Joe died at 47 Railway Street, Newcastle.

He was 33.

On February 17 he was buried, in Jesmond Old Cemetery - Plot 5K, Ward 7 - attended by:

Two mourning coaches.

A dozen cabs, and...

Thousands of mourners on foot.

*Dawn and Daryl enter.*

**DAWN:** (*angry*) Arguably the greatest Geordie singer/songwriter buried in an unmarked grave!

**DARYL:** Aye.

**DAWN:** Where did all the money go then? Don't answer that! And why did it take Allan 15 years to buy Joe a headstone?

**DARYL:** Well, Allan had another book of Joe's songs coming out.

**DAWN:** Ah, a marketing scam!

**DARYL:** I read somewhere the profit on the book was four times more than the cost of the headstone. But it could just be a total coincidence!

**DAWN:** Look, a flying pig!

**DARYL:** Sadly, Bella was back at the cemetery two months later. Eight-month-old Robert died of bronchitis - he was buried next to his dad.

**DAWN:** Poor Bella. How old was she when Joe and Robert died?

**DARYL:** 23.

*Johnny enters.*

**JOHNNY:** Sorry, guys. I had to gan y'hem - forgot me tabs, didn't I?

*They all look at him.*

**JOHNNY:** *(looks around)* Have I missed much?

**DAWN:** I'm away to get changed.

*Dawn and Daryl exiting.*

**DARYL:** In the spring of 1879, Bella, the children and her mother emigrated - sailed from Liverpool to Quebec.

*They exit.*

*Johnny picks up the book.*

**JOHNNY:** Canada by sea? I wouldn't fancy that, mind.

**PHIL:** Aye, the North Shields ferry's bad enough.

**JOHNNY:** Think yourself lucky, man, I get seasick on the boats at Marine Park.

*He and Johnny laugh.*

**JOHNNY:** (*reading book*) This bit's underlined - does it mean owt to you, Phil? Between Joe dying and Bella emigrating, she went back on stage...as Mrs Joe Wilson.

*Bella enters to applause.*

**BELLA:** Thank you. This song is dedicated to anyone missing a loved one.

*Bella sings Charley's Across The Sea.*

**BELLA:** Sadly aw sing, for me sweetheart's away
Over the sea, he's been mony a day;
Mony a day, he's been pairted frae me
Leaving us grieving for him on the sea.

(*chorus*) Bonny bright moon, send Charley te me
Myek his path leet an' safe on the sea;
Shine on, ye stars, an' sparkle as free
Charley's across the sea.

Often aw've thowt i' the lang weary neet
The moon an' the stars wad keep Charley reet;
Withoot them aw fancy an' dreed thor's a storm
An' Charley's i' danger, ne mair he'll return.

(*chorus*)

Then shine on, bright moon, byeth radiant an' warm
Keep Charley frae danger, keep him free frae harm;
An' brighten his pathway se wild on the sea,
An' send back me sweetheart, me Charley, te me-

*She's upset and exits to chords of the song, which continue long enough for Bella to exit.*

*Lights up.*

*Present time. Setting up for Joe Wilson Night.*

*Johnny moves to the Joe Wilson standing placard.*

*Daryl enters in morning jacket and bow tie.*

*Phil puts poster on front of his piano and quietly directs the raising of the large Newcastle City Blue Plaque.*

*Dawn enters. Daryl and Dawn use the chest as a prop to put things in as they talk.*

**DARYL:** Bella took three children to America, you know. She gave birth to a daughter, Mary Annie, in 1879 - four years after Joe died.

**DAWN:** There's nothing wrong with an unmarried woman having sex!

**DARYL:** I know...but...Mary Annie's father was Tom!

*She drops the chest lid on Daryl's hand. (owww!).*

**DAWN:** Tom? What, Joe's brother Tom?

**DARYL:** Tom, aye.

**DAWN:** You're joking!

**JOHNNY:** *(with standing placard)* Hey, can you give iz a hand to turn this around?

**DARYL:** Bella remarried in 1881. She was 30 and now known as Isabella Frederick. She had three more children.

**JOHNNY:** Are you going to give iz a hand, or what, man?

**DARYL:** Bella died in Michigan, 1930. Aged 80.

**DAWN:** What about Tom?

**DARYL:** Tom? He died in 1912 in Newcastle, aged 70. Buried in All Saints Cemetery, Jesmond.

**JOHNNY:** I'll do it myself, shall I?

*Johnny turns the frame around and takes the cover off to reveal the picture of Joe Wilson.*

**DARYL:** Ellen, Tom's wife, outlived them all - she died in 1932, aged 87.

**DAWN:** I wonder if she knew about Mary Annie.

*Stage set for show.*

**JOHNNY:** Right, are we ready to rock?

**DAWN/DARYL/PHIL:** Aye/yes.

**JOHNNY:** I'll tell them to let people in.

*Johnny exits.*

**DAWN:** Eh, Daryl.

**DARYL:** What?

**DAWN:** Sorry about, you know, the phone message earlier.

**DARYL:** It's all right, man - you're me sister, me favourite sister.

**DAWN:** Ahhh (*realises*) Hey, I'm your only sister!

*She hits him. They laugh as they exit.*

*Daryl limps.*

**DAWN:** Do not do the walk.

**DARYL:** All right, all right.

*They exit.*

*Johnny enters.*

**JOHNNY:** Ladies and gentlemen, welcome to Joe Wilson Night, to celebrate the birth of the man who was to become the Bard of the North East, not just Tyneside. Please give a warm welcome for the great Joe Wilson.

*Daryl and Dawn enter as chords of Keep Yor Feet Still play.*

**DARYL:** Hello everybody. Now, this is a homely sang I think you'll aal knaa. I hope you're ganna join in the chorus, mind.

*Daryl, Dawn and Johnny sing Keep Yor Feet Still!*

**DARYL:** Wor Geordey an' Bob Jonsin byeth lay i' one bed,
Iv a little lodgjin hoose that's doon the shore,
Before Bob had been an' oor asleep, a kick frae Geordey's

fut myed him wakin up te roar instead o' snore.

**ALL:** (*chorus*) "Keep yor feet still! Geordey, hinny, let's be happy for the neet, For aw maynit be se happy throo the day. So give us that bit cumfort, keep yor feet still, Geordey lad, An' dinnet send maw bonny dreams away!"

**JOHNNY:** Aw dreamt thor was a dancin held, an' Mary Clark wes there; An' aw thowt we tript it leetly on the floor, An' aw prest her heevin breest te mine when walsin roond the room, That's mair than aw dor ivor de before.

**ALL:** (*chorus*)

**DARYL:** Ye'll knaw the lad that she gans with, they call him Jimmy Green, Aw thowt he tried te spoil us i' wor fun, But aw dreamt aw nail'd him heavy, an' blackt the big feul's eyes; If aw'd slept it's hard to tell what aw wad deun

**ALL:** (*chorus*)

**DAWN:** Aw thowt aw set her hyem that neet, content we went alang. Aw kiss'd her lips a hundrid times or mair, An' aw wish'd the road wad nivor end, se happy like wes aw, Aw cud walk'd a thoosind miles wi' Mary there!

**ALL:** (*chorus*)

**DARYL:** Aw dremt Jim Green had left the toon an' left his luv te me, An' aw thowt the hoose wis furnish'd wi' the best.

*They expect the audience to sing.*

*Music stops.*

**DARYL:** (*speaks to audience*) Whoah, whoah, what happened there? Back in the day, when Joe used to sing this song there was audience participation, like this (*sings*) Aw dremt Jim Green had left the toon an' left his luv te me, An' aw thowt the hoose wis furnish'd wi' the best.

...the audience would shout "all on tick"...yes? Can you do that?....Ok (*sings unaccompanied*) An' aw thowt the hoose wis furnish'd wi' the best *(audience sings "all on tick")* ... brilliant ...*(to pianist)* Hit it maestro ...

*Music starts.*

**DARYL:** (*sings*) Aw dremt Jim Green had left the toon an' left his luv te me, An' aw thowt the hoose wis furnish'd wi' the best [all on tick] An' aw dreamt aw just had left the church wi' Mary be me side, When yor clumsy feet completely spoil'd the rest.

**ALL:** (*chorus*) Keep yor feet still! Geordey, hinny, let's be happy for the neet, For aw maynit be se happy throo the day.

**PHIL:** (*sings*) Through the day.

*They look at Phil. Music stops.*

**ALL:** (*to Phil*) Shut up. (*slower*) So give us that bit cumfort, keep yor feet still, Geordey lad, An' dinnet send maw bonny dreams awayyyyyy!

*Applause.*

**DAWN:** Thank you.

**DARYL:** Does anyone have to catch their last bus home? Do you want some more songs? Are you sure?

OK, hit it, Phil.

*They sing a brief medley of songs with Johnny on guitar. This includes The Chep That Knas Nowt, Hannah's Black Eye, Row iv a Public Hoose, Dinnet Clash The Door, The Miseries o' Shiftin', Sally Wheatley and Keep Yor Feet Still. (end the show on the chorus).*

*Applause.*

*The cast saluting the Joe Wilson standing placard.*

*The lights go down.*

## THE END

# CARRYING
# DAVID

# ACT ONE

One Man Cast

*The action takes place on a plain stage with screen projections. The props comprise a bar table, bar stool, a bottle of whisky, a glass and a scrapbook. The directorial instructions are for guidance only.*

*Lights down.*

*The last pre-show song we hear is The Boxer by Simon and Garfunkel.*

**S&G:** I am just a poor boy Though my story's seldom told
I have squandered my resistance
For a pocketful of mumbles
Such are promises
All lies and jest
Still, a man hears what he wants to hear
And disregards the rest.

(*lights going down*) La, la, la, la, la, la, la, la, la, la, la.

*The song segues into the final verse of The Boxer.*

**S&G:** (*song*) In the clearing stands a boxer, and a fighter by his trade.

*Glenn enters in a suit and T-shirt and sits at the table. He pours himself some whisky and occasionally sips it.*

**S&G:** And he carries the reminders of every glove that laid him down or cut him till he cried out
in his anger and his shame I am leaving, I am leaving but the fighter still remains, lie, la, lie *(fades)*

*Image on screen: David McCrory.*

*Lights up.*

**GLENN:** Have you ever watched programmes like *Question Time* and wanted to kick the telly because the people on it are talking rubbish?

In contrast, I grew up watching Parkinson - the Ali interviews *(as Ali)* I am the greatest *(normal)* inspirational.

Watching Ali, I would dream of being a world champion boxer. Ali's was a good story...mine isn't bad either.

**INTERVIEWER (V/O):** So Glenn, you were crowned International Boxing Federation Cruiserweight champion of the world in June 1989, which you held for ten months, successfully defending it once...and then you were a Sky television boxing presenter for...

**GLENN:** 27 years.

**INTERVIEWER (V/O):** Do you, um, miss getting your head pummelled?

**GLENN:** Well, put it this way, I've much preferred watching the likes of Lennox Lewis, Floyd Mayweather and Manny Pacquiao from the safe side of the ropes.

**INTERVIEWER (V/O):** And you've been an actor.

**GLENN:** Yes. Theatre and television - I wouldn't mind giving acting another go, though.

**INTERVIEWER (V/O):** Since your title win you've had your fair share of setbacks.

**GLENN:** Aye, I was declared bankrupt not long after and twice divorced...but I've got two beautiful children with my long-term partner, making it five in total.

**INTERVIEWER (V/O):** You're a grandfather as well, aren't, you?

**GLENN:** I've got two grand-daughters older than my son!

**INTERVIEWER (V/O):** And where does your brother David fit into your story?

**GLENN:** David was my inspiration.

**INTERVIEWER (V/O):** Now, tell me about your background.

**GLENN:** Well, I was born in Annfield Plain near Stanley.

**INTERVIEWER (V/O):** Stanley who?

**GLENN:** It's in County Durham.

**INTERVIEWER (V/O):** You'll have to narrow it down. Where is it near?

**GLENN:** No Place.

**INTERVIEWER (V/O):** It's got to be somewhere.

**GLENN:** Pity Me.

**INTERVIEWER (V/O):** I do son, I do.

**GLENN:** Pity Me, No Place - they're villages *(beat)* Look, Annfield Plain is in County Durham - to the North is the fantastic metropolis of Newcastle, to the east is the wonderful city of Sunderland, to the south is the beautiful, historic city of Durham and to the West is, um...Shotley Bridge.

**INTERVIEWER (V/O):** Now Glenn, would you say yours was the usual road to the top?

**GLENN:** Oh aye, textbook. *(privileged accent)* Mummy and daddy lined up a top prep school, then 12 years at boarding school...followed by Oxbridge...and, through the old school tie, a crack at the world title, ha, ha.

*(looks at audience)* What are you laughing at?

I was the third of six siblings. In case you're wondering, yes, we are Catholics. I wore hand-me-downs, we lived in a three-bedroom rented house with broken windows and I shared a bed with my two brothers until I was 18 - that's why I've always slept with my underpants on!

*On screen: "seconds out, Round 1. Being Glenn McCrory".*

*Takes jacket off.*

**MALE (V/O):** Seconds out Round 1. Being Glenn McCrory.

**GLENN:** *(standing, animated)* You hear it all the time, don't you? Despite being from a council estate...despite attending a comprehensive school...let me tell you this, it's because of my background that I became the world champion..."because" - only one word but with vast connotations.

My father worked at Consett steelworks - he had a debilitating accident there...my mam was a housewife...her four brothers died from diseases directly related to working in the mines. (*laughs*) As a young kid I thought my uncles were black - all I ever saw were their coaly faces when they came home from work!

I wasn't brave enough to follow them down the pit - but, for a 16-year-old working class lad in 1980...(*to audience member*) Stop counting on your fingers pet, I was born in September 1964.

...my career prospect was a lifetime of manual work in the mines, steel mills or shipyards. But I was determined to do something different, not to forget where I come from! No, just do something different.

*On screen: "Seconds out Round 2. March 1974".*

**MALE (V/O):** Seconds out Round 2. March 1974.

*Image: David McCrory.*

**GLENN:** (*as 9-year-old*) Mam, mam, there's a strange boy in my bed.

**MAM (V/O):** It's, um, David's bed now, Glenn.

**GLENN:** What? Eh? Where will I sleep?

**MAM (V/O):** With your brothers, love.

**GLENN:** Hadaway! There's already two of them in the double bed.

**MAM (V/O):** Gary and Shaun don't mind.

**GLENN:** But I do! (*points*) That's my bed. (*to audience*) The person in what was my bottom bunk was David - and I didn't like him. He wore National Health glasses and walked funny, like this...

*Shows David's way of walking.*

**GLENN:** ...and if we wanted extra biscuits off mam, like this.

*Feigns really difficult walking.*

**GLENN:** (*laughs*) But that was later. David was born on March 2, 1966. He was living at Nazareth House, an orphanage in Newcastle.

He'd had a couple of foster families, neither had worked out. Instrumental in the adoption was Father Phelan, who thought that despite having six kids already, mam and dad would give David a chance in life...and my bed!

With the addition of David, the 9-strong McCrorys - 10 if you count the dog - weren't so much a family...we were a tribe (*beat*) Close friends.

But as a child I felt like an outsider.

Gary was the first born - and first-borns tend to be the apple of their parents' eye.

Next came Karen, the oldest girl.

Neil, my younger brother, had hearing difficulties and was given special attention.

Then the twins - Kelly and Sean, well twins are always special, aren't they?

And now David had come along.

This left me with a sense that I was the only one who didn't have anything unique about him. (*shouts*) Hello! Can anybody see me? Hello. I'm here. Hello!

As I was the closest in age to David, I seemed to be stuck with him all the time...that really pissed me off an'all. We attended St Patrick's school together - it involved a long walk up a hill. David's slowness meant we were often late and I kept getting the cane.

*Holds hand out.*

**GLENN:** But it's not my fault, sir.

*Thwak! (sound of cane).*

**GLENN:** Owwwwww!

*He rubs his hand.*

**GLENN:** (*points to David*) This is your fault...

*He is running to school but David is holding him up.*

**GLENN:** (*to David*) Come on - we're going to be late again

...run faster.

*Glenn runs a couple of steps but comes back to David.*

**GLENN:** *(shouts)* Hurry up. I'm sick of you - you're always holding me back.

*(to David)* Don't tell me to sod off...sod off yourself...no you sod off...I don't care if you said it first, I said it second.

*(panicking)* Three minutes 'til the bell.

*He's torn between leaving David and helping him.*

**GLENN:** That's when I picked David up...and put him on my back.

*He's carrying David.*

**GLENN:** *(to David)* Hang on tight.

*Glenn runs with David on back.*

**GLENN:** David started laughing...it felt good.

Faster?

You want to go faster? *(shouts)* Hold on, then.

We were weaving between pupils, scattering them aside.

*Glenn runs and weaves.*

*Sound of child giggling.*

**GLENN:** He giggled. I giggled.

(*shouts*) Get out the way. Ahhhhhhhhh!

I started hopping, skipping and jumping.

*Glenn hops, skips and jumps.*

**GLENN:** David laughed louder...so I hopped and skipped more...

*Glenn hops, skips and jumps.*

**GLENN:** ...and the more I jumped around the more he laughed. Everyone was looking at us but we didn't care. We were having great fun. We were going to beat the bell...but I didn't want this to end...it was exciting, absolutely brilliant ...(*excited*) truly exhilarating!

Then I felt David's lips on my cheek.

(*to David*) How man, stop slavering on iz.

But he did it again and...I realised he'd ...

*He stops and touches cheek.*

**GLENN:** He'd kissed me. The laughter stopped.

*He puts David down.*

**GLENN:** I put him down...this small, dishevelled boy standing in front of me was in tears...he said that was longest anyone had ever held him.

Wey, that set me off, didn't it? We both stood there bubbling...we must have looked like a right pair of soft tits.

The school bell went and I was late, again. (*laughs*) I got the cane, didn't I? (*rubs hand*) But I didn't care. It still bloody hurt, though. (*laughs*).

I know all of us had their own special relationship with David, but our lifelong connection had been forged.

One day a kid at school called David a "spacker" - so I punched the living daylights out of him.

I'm not proud of it...

*Glenn waves his hand and smiles.*

**GLENN:** ...but no one was going to pick on my family. It never happened again!

*Image: "Round 3. Learning the Ropes".*

**MALE (V/O):** Seconds out Round 3. Learning the ropes.

*Bell rings.*

**GLENN:** My grandfather had been an army champion and my great uncle had fought for the Empire title, so we've got a tradition of boxing in our family.

In 1976 I was tall and physically strong for my age - but it was a skinny 12-year-old who joined Consett Sports Centre boxing club.

Around 25 kids in shorts, boots and vests were either skipping (*skips*) hitting bags (*punches*) and sparring (*spars*)...oh, man, it was magical.

To pay for the membership and my equipment I flogged my free school meal vouchers and went, um, foraging... (*secretively*) next time you go to Beamish Museum - look at the old Annfield Plain Co-op...you can hardly call it a real crime if the lead was left lying around on a building site, can you? (*taps nose*) We'll say no more.

*Glenn shadow boxes through this next bit and does the appropriate actions.*

**GLENN:** I trained at the boxing club two days a week (*he jabs*) jab, jab, jab.

The rest of the time I'd push the chairs back in the sitting room.

(*he punches*) One-two, one-two (*he uppercuts*) Uppercut.

You have to train every day if you want to become champion of the world, David.

(*he stops*) You know, when I said that to David he never sniggered...he never doubted it, not once.

(*moves*) Move in...to the stomach. (*he punches*)

Some days dad wore the pads.

*He punches hard.*

**GLENN:** Some days mam wore the pads.

*He pulls back from hitting her.*

**GLENN:** Um, no.

Some days I asked David to wear the pads.

*Glenn chases David off stage, trying to land punches.*

**GLENN:** Stand still, man - come back!

(*he boxes*) Some days I practised defensive moves.

Inside parry. (*action*).

(*he boxes*) David and me would listen to Ali's fights on the transistor radio under the bed sheets.

Outside parry. (*action*).

(*he boxes*) We bought cine reels and flickered them on the dodgy 1970s bedroom Anaglypta wallpaper.

(*he stops, to audience*) Some of you posher ones might have had woodchip.

Ali taking out Sonny Liston (*punches*) bang...and Cleveland Williams (*punches*) bang, bang, bang. Joe Louis against Buddy Baer and his famous knockout of Max Schmeling...whack! (*punches*) Fights featuring Ezzard Charles and (*does shuffle*) Jersey Joe Walcott, who was doing the shuffle before The Greatest was born.
Block the jab! (*does action*)

(*he shows following moves*) Inside elbow, outside elbow, block-guard!

Stay focused at all times.

While others had pictures of Malcolm MacDonald, Bobby

Kerr or Abba on their bedroom walls, mine were of boxing legends.

*Images: Rocky Marciano, Muhammad Ali, Joe Frazier, George Foreman and Teofilo Stevenson follow in quick succession.*

**GLENN:** Rocky Marciano, Muhammad Ali, Joe Frazier, George Foreman, Teófilo Stevenson.

I'd devour books about boxing and the great boxers. I bought *The Ring* magazine and *Boxing News*. I also read Dylan Thomas, Dante...and my favourite, Oscar Wilde. (*as Wilde*) We are all in the gutter, dear boy, but some of us are looking at the stars.

(*shuffles*) Moving your feet so you're always well balanced.

*He stops.*

**GLENN:** This was my education, not school.

David and me could name every world heavyweight champion and British champ in any weight division. One day I too was going to hear the roar of the crowd as I was lifted shoulder high.

*We hear a crowd sound.*

(*Glenn commentates as he boxes*) And it's McCrory on top...he jabs (*he jabs*)...oh that is beautiful boxing...(*excited*) he lands with a one-two (*he punches*)...oh, my god, Ali is down...it's a sensation...15-year-old Glenn McCrory has knocked out The Greatest.

*Sound of loud cheers and Glenn holds up his arms in victory.*

*The sound stops abruptly.*

**GLENN:** But first I had to actually fight! There are two types of boxing - amateur and professional. Amateur is three, three-minute rounds...and you wear a vest for recognition...not because it's cold in the ring!

In professional boxing you progress up to 12 three-minute rounds and hopefully compete for a world title shot in glamorous...Las Vegas.

My boxing debut took place on October 6, 1979, a fortnight after my 15th birthday.

A working men's club in Witton Gilbert...the Las Vegas of the North! Except with more glamour! The whole McCrory tribe was there. For the occasion I wore new, proper blue boots. Mam had customised my dressing gown.

*On screen: A dressing gown containing "McCrory" in crappy wording.*

**GLENN:** She'd ironed the letters on! A points victory after three rounds - yes! By February 1980 I'd won five out of five and then bagged *(takes deep breath)* The North East District Junior Amateur Boxing Association title. Saying that was harder than the fight!

My picture was in the *Stanley News*...I was a contender! David cut it out and put it in his new scrapbook. It was around this time that I started courting Mandy - we were at school together. One minute we were all "sweet 16"...the next...*(shouts)* I'm not giving up boxing, right! Why would I want to give up on my dream?

*On screen: Image of Crawford Ashley.*

**GLENN:** Six months in, my eighth bout was against Leeds-based Crawford Ashley in the North Eastern Counties Amateur Championship.

I lost on points but Ashley later turned pro and became British, Commonwealth and European Light-Heavyweight Champion - it was a mark of how far I'd come in such a short time.

The season after, I reached the final of the North Eastern Counties ABA Championship. But the run-up hadn't been too great.

*Image: David.*

**GLENN:** *(to mam)* Mam, are you all right? What's wrong? Why are you crying? Mam? *(beat)* Friedreich's what? Ataxia?

*(to audience)* We'd noticed David's feet turning inwards and his walking was getting worse.

*(looks at David image)* What mam and dad didn't tell us was that the doctors gave David six months to live...he was only 15!

The degenerative disease also affected his throat...one day at the dinner table, in mid conversation, David started choking ...dad revived him, sat him back at the table and we continued the conversation as if nothing had happened.

Mandy's jaw dropped; she couldn't understand what had just

happened. For us it had become normal.

For David, it must have been horrendous.

Mandy headed off to Germany to work.

And on May 29, 1981...

**MAN (V/O):** The new Great Britain Junior ABA champion...Glenn McCrory.

**GLENN:** British Amateur Champion! Only 20 months since that heady night in Witton Gilbert.

At last I could shout (*shouts*) I'm here, I exist. I'm not invisible!

David got excited when fight nights were approaching... always asking questions, questions, questions. Who have you been sparring with? Did you work on your jab? Can I come to the fight? When will you be in the *Stanley News* again? Bla, bla, bla, bla, bla.

The truth was, I needed David as much as he needed me... and I loved all the bla, bla, blaring.

In February 1982 I travelled to Oslo as part of a North East Select team. David, meanwhile, had moved to the Cedars, a special school in Gateshead.

He was provided with a stair lift at home, which meant no one walked up stairs again - even the neighbours came in to try it! And David got a wheelchair...well, he was strapped in it while we perfected all sorts of wheelies and other death-defying feats.

*Glenn pushes invisible wheelchair.*

**GLENN:** Wheeeeeeeeeeeeee...dogs fled (*dog barks*) and lamp-posts were often hit (*crash sound*).

*Glenn laughs.*

**GLENN:** So here I was, flying to Norway! The furthest and most exotic place I've been to was a bus ride to Blackpool on a family caravan holiday. I fought a Norwegian senior international. I lost a close points decision - but what an experience for someone who'd just turned 17. Next, I was called up to the senior England Under-19 squad - the youngest member - training with...

*On screen: Images of Errol Christie, Duke McKenzie and Chris Pyatt in succession.*

**GLENN:** ...Errol Christie...Duke McKenzie and Chris Pyatt, who between them would win British, European and world professional titles.

Next thing I know I'm part of a Great Britain Select team in New York...not the one next to North Shields - but the Big Apple...my progress was rapid.

Dare I whisper it...*(whisper loud)* the 1984 Los Angeles Olympics? Don't make me laugh!

The *(privileged accent)* old school British selectors *(normal accent)* back then picked experienced guys rather than teenage upstarts.

Between you and me, had I been selected for the 1984 Games I would have run into a young heavyweight called

Evander Holyfield.

*On screen: Holyfield.*

**GLENN:** Perhaps it was for the best! Those of you who don't know who Evander Holyfield is, he's one of the greatest boxers of all time but he's now missing some of his ear thanks to Mike Tyson. More about those two later.

My amateur record was 56 wins and only 10 defeats. For a teenager fighting seniors it was a proud record...he said, modestly.

*On screen: "Round 4. Mixing with the Big Boys".*

**MALE (V/O):** Seconds out. Round 4. Mixing with the big boys.

*Bell rings.*

**GLENN:** Returning from New York in late 1983, soon after my 19th birthday, I turned professional. With hindsight, a sponsor and a career plan would have made life easier, a lot easier.

(*as an adviser*) Right Glenn, here's the score...you're going for gold at the 1988 Olympics - you'll still only be 23 - turn professional and we can make some serious money.

I actually won the world cruiserweight title less than a year after the 1988 Olympics...and my house got repossessed...for the second time...but that's 20-20 hindsight for you.

Professional boxing in the North East had always been too

far north for the London-based promoters and trainers...and so, to the bright lights of the Old Smoke I headed.

*On screen: Doug Bidwell.*

**DOUG (V/O):** (*Cockney*) You awright?

**GLENN:** With greased back hair, he looked like Del Boy - he even had the gold sovereign rings.

He took dad and me to a swanky restaurant...well anything that wasn't a Burger King was swanky for me back then.

**DOUG (V/O):** (*Cockney*) I managed Alan Minter to the world Middleweight title, Mr MaGrory [SIC].

I am going to train your boy and place the heavyweight crown on his head.

**GLENN:** Oh, man! A new, glamorous world opened up. (*excited*) Hob-nobbing with television and film stars, five-star hotels, limousines...Versace suits...super models throwing themselves at me...and (*he pretends to forget this lines, the more uncomfortable for the audience the better*)...and...sorry, sorry...I have to go back a bit, sorry.

Rewind.

*Glenn rewinds.*

**GLENN:** A new, glamorous world opened up...Doug Bidwell paid me nothing for signing with him. He placed me in a pokey B&B...a single bed that was too small. The old wife who ran the place had cancer - she smoked and coughed all the time.

For breakfast I got one egg...one egg, and a single slice of bacon. I spent my dole money...yes dole money...on food. The only limousines I saw were those that splashed water on me. Doug couldn't even say my name right... MaGrory...I ask you!

(*to audience*) What was the name of that bloke who went to London in search of gold...um, Whittington, aye that's him (*to audience*) What was his first name? [DICK].

Aye, that was me, a complete dick!

Minter actually had a brilliant trainer called Bobby Neill. Doug Bidwell had managed but never trained a fighter in his life. He wanted that Holy Grail of boxing at the time - a white British heavyweight world champion.

I was his guinea pig!

The truth is I was little more than a big, light-heavyweight.

I trained at the famous Thomas A Becket gym on the Old Kent Road - Ali had trained there...and Sugar Ray Robinson.

Skint and miserable, I missed everyone at home. Lonely night followed lonely night. I particularly missed David. We spoke regularly on the phone.

He told me Mandy had returned from Germany. I hadn't seen her for the best part of a year. I was confused. I often looked at bus timetables - I could leave London any time... for what, though?

Every time the doubts engulfed me, David would be there, on my shoulder. You can't quit...why are you even thinking this? You've got a chance, Glenn!

My last fight as an amateur I weighed 12 stone 7 - a light-heavyweight...but Doug would say...

**DOUG (V/O):** You're growing; you're going to be a heavyweight and we're going to build you up into one.

**GLENN:** In an attempt to reach 14st 5lb - nearly two stones heavier than my natural weight - Doug had me constantly eating bacon and sausages...washed down with gold top milk...a balanced diet - fat and fat.

*Bell rings.*

**GLENN:** My professional debut.

Doug put me - a 19-year-old debutant - in with Barry Ellis, an undefeated heavyweight...more than a stone heavier than me. I'd never actually seen a live professional fight...this was my first - and I was in it!

I looked across at this huge guy.

*He looks up.*

**GLENN:** I feared for my life...I swear!

*He crosses himself.*

**GLENN:** David, I'd see you in heaven.

*He covers.*

*Bell rings rapidly.*

**GLENN:** The fight was over after 90 seconds.

The next day *The Sun*, under a caption "The White Bruno?" featured a picture of me with the phrase...(*Cockney*) The sweetest left hook since Henry Cooper. I'd thrown punches out of sheer terror and caught him...a first round knock out!

Two weeks later...I'm up against another unbeaten heavyweight.

(*to Doug*) Eight rounds at the Albert Hall? You're joking, Doug!

I won on points.

Next fight I suffered my first cut eye - but not from a punch. Southpaws, you see, unorthodox...leading with the right...

*He moves southpaw style.*

**GLENN:** ...miss with a jab, they slip inside and bang...heads connect! I won a points decision after six rounds.

I'm now entering the ring at Grosvenor House in Mayfair, London...

*Enters between ropes.*

**GLENN:** ...and I glimpse at the top table.

*He stands mouth agape.*

**GLENN:** There, no more than ten yards away, staring at me...gawping at him (*awestruck*) M...Mu...Muhammad Ali...I didn't need to double take, the greatest had no lookalikes.

The fight was now secondary - how was I going to show this man I loved him?

The bell went.

What did I do?

The Ali shuffle, that's what!

And then I raised my hand above my head - Ali style.

*Shuffling, hand raised.*

*His smile turns to shock.*

*He stops.*

**GLENN:** Oh, my god! What if The Greatest thought I was taking the piss?

I won a points decision over six rounds. After the fight *(towel to face in embarrassment)*, ahhhhhh...I'm sitting in the changing room thinking what a total prick I'd been when...

*Image: Glenn and Ali.*

*He looks up.*

**GLENN:** Ali walked in I said "goodness me" *(beat)* Or words to that effect. He said: *(as Ali)* Maaaan you're gonna be champion of the world one day but cut that shit out!

*They shake hands.*

**GLENN:** Yes Mr Ali, sir. I hoped some of his greatness had rubbed off on me - I never washed that hand for a week!

To Wales next...when does a teenage heavyweight fight six times in four months?

Crazy!

*Glenn shows the following.*

**GLENN:** My favourite move was the left, right, left combination. It was my speed that kept me out of trouble against bigger opponents and enabled me to win on points.

I'd get a £1,000 purse.

**DOUG (V/O):** £750 for me, £250 for you.

**GLENN:** What?

The dole would stop my giro for a couple of weeks until the purse money was gone and then I'd be signing on again. While feeding me fatty fry ups, Doug would arrange sparring with experienced fighters.

*On screen: James Smith, Trevor Berbick and Gerrie Coetzee accompany their names.*

**GLENN:** James "Bonecrusher" Smith before his world title eliminator with Frank Bruno.

Trevor Berbick.

Gerrie Coetzee.

Men who soon after went on to be world heavyweight champions.

Despite wearing protection, it was painful and totally inappropriate work for a 19-year-old novice at least two stone lighter than them.

In September 1984 I turned 20.

Doug reasoned:

**DOUG (V/O):** Make a name for yourself in your home area and we could really start to make some money.

**GLENN:** I had a three fights on Tyneside - in 11 weeks!

*Glenn reflects and shakes head.*

**GLENN:** Nine professional fights in nine months. Admittedly, Bruno fought ten fights in his first nine months - but he fought only 17 rounds in total...against opponents brought in to be knocked out! I fought 55 rounds...55 hard rounds against bigger men.

At least David had more pictures for his scrapbook. By now he was dependent on his wheelchair...even his speaking had deteriorated. Mam, I knew, often shed tears...but being mam she was selfless...David, being David, just smiled...ever eager to share in my success...while he continued to beat the odds.

I never got in touch with Mandy on my return to the North East. I reasoned we weren't an item any more.

I was at mam's house. She handed me the phone...it was Mandy's mam. She told me Mandy was seriously ill in

Durham Hospital. I rushed there with Father Phelan, who gave Mandy the last rites.

I was distraught and confused...our relationship had been tumultuous - one minute we were together, the next we weren't - one minute she wanted me to give up boxing the next she didn't.

Luckily Mandy recovered.

How could I break-up with her now?

Six months later I went to see Father Phelan who said (*as Father Phelan*) You don't have to marry Mandy, Glenn.

But she's pregnant!

We married on June 1, 1985.

We were 20 years old.

Although my boxing career had been going well - and a fight had been televised - the truth was, we didn't even have money for a honeymoon. Helped by my sister Karen, we bought a little house in Annfield Plain - but I didn't have the money to pay the mortgage every month.

Then Doug had another of his great ideas!

**DOUG (V/O):** We're going to the States.

**GLENN:** He touted me as this young, undefeated British heavyweight.

*Image: Larry Holmes.*

**GLENN:** I visited the Larry Holmes camp as he prepared for his world title defence against David Bey. Holmes was a double Heavyweight belt holder...undefeated in 12 years.

He beat Bey in ten rounds.

*Image: Glenn with Holmes.*

**GLENN:** To be in such rarefied company was incredible.

*On screen: Images of Randall Cobb and Mike Dokes.*

**GLENN:** Doug sparred me with Randall 'Tex' Cobb and Mike Dokes - both world title contenders. But Doug was no Don King or Frank Warren - there was no long-term strategy.

*Image: "Round 5: The Outcast".*

**MALE (V/O):** Seconds out Round 5. The outcast.

**GLENN:** September 1985, three weeks before my 21st birthday.

On the dole and worrying how to pay the bills, I took on Newcastle heavyweight John Westgarth at Gateshead Leisure Centre in North East England – home. Thanks to Doug's so-called training regime I weighed in at 14 stone 8 - my heaviest ever. I was carrying 18 pounds of excess fat.

*Bell sounds.*

**GLENN:** I felt slow and cumbersome. Despite this, I boxed well in the early stages. John was 6ft 5, strong and wild. If I could keep moving and use my jab I would handle him with no real difficulty. After three rounds of jabbing, Doug screamed:

**DOUG (V/O):** Take him out! Take him out! He's gone!

**GLENN:** Bollocks! He was still as strong as an ox and throwing me about in the clinches. I went into the fourth round, jabbing, jabbing, jabbing.

Doug's screaming:

**DOUG (V/O):** Make a name for yourself, knock him out...knock him out.

**GLENN:** Then a moment of indecision...should I?

Boom!

*Glenn takes a right hook and falls to the floor.*

**COMMENTARY (V/O):** And Westgarth lands with a vicious right hook...McCrory is on the canvass.

*Glenn gets up, slowly.*

**GLENN:** I wasn't hurt but I was heading for defeat.

The crowd erupted.

*Crowd cheering.*

**GLENN:** That moment...that awful moment...I thought the whole of my beloved North East was against me - forget London, this was the loneliest time of my life.

They though I was the unbeaten fancy Dan from London...they thought I'd sold them out for fame and wealth. Apart from the birth of my daughter, Victoria, in November 1985, the next year was the bleakest of my life.

I moved back home, signed on the dole and trained on my own...the domestic arguments followed a similar pattern...(*shouts*) I've got a proper job...alright, alright!

I even went for interviews at the Job Centre.

**OFFICE WORKER (V/O):** Now Mr McCrory, what would you like to do?

**GLENN:** Win a world boxing title.

*Image: "Round 6: A Boxing Whore".*

**MALE (V/O):** Seconds out Round 6. A boxing whore.

**GLENN:** Realising he didn't have a potential world champion, Doug now matched me wherever he could earn a few quid.

*Image: Glenn fighting Pika.*

**GLENN:** The unbeaten Welsh heavyweight southpaw Rudi Pika at the Albert Hall...a close, hard eight-round fight.

**ANNOUNCER (V/O):** The judges score Pika 79 points to McCrory's 77 and a half.

**GLENN:** My second defeat.

Nine days later...nine days later! I'm in Denmark facing the former European Heavyweight Champion Anders Eklund.

*On screen: Anders Eklund.*

**GLENN:** Eklund - 6ft 7 - had been European Heavyweight Champion until he lost his crown to Frank Bruno six months earlier.

A third defeat.

Constant money worries, arguments with Mandy, coping with a new baby - the pressures added to my woes.

*On screen: Dave Garside.*

**GLENN:** Next I faced Dave Garside in Blackpool.

Round seven.

I felt I was out-boxing him...then (*he nuts*). The referee gave him a warning. I was cut. And then he nutted me again... bang - a clear head-butt. Blood flowed from the cut. The referee give him a final warning and then...

**COMMENTARY (V/O):** The referee's looking at McCrory's left eye...he's stopped the fight...my goodness.

**GLENN:** It was an absolute scandal.

*Glenn moves to sit on edge of stage.*

**GLENN:** The next day I received a telegram.

"You may have lost a fight but you will win the war. I am a fan".

(*looks up*) Thank you Les Dawson.

But back in the North East with no resources, no trainer, no facilities...no hope...no inspiration...it was a desperate time. The darkness descends...you begin to question your very existence.

What is the purpose of my life?

Why does David cling to his life?

Even my ever-loyal dad was concerned for me. Whenever there was a problem with us kids, it was dad who got the job to talk to us - and it always started: "Your mam and me..."

*He stands.*

**GLENN:** So, with the repo man circling the house I foolishly agreed to fight...

*On screen: Hughroy Currie.*

**GLENN:** ...Hughroy Currie.

Two days before the bout - (*shakes head in resignation*) two days - Mandy put on the pads and I trained in our kitchen.

*Looks at image.*

**GLENN:** That was my preparation against a recently deposed, big and powerful, British heavyweight champion. From an undefeated prospect to a no-hoper in less than a year!

Worse, I'd become a boxing whore.

I went into the ring 15 stone 6 - a career high.

My mobility deserted me...I was never a slogger.

Second round...bang!

**COMMENTATOR (V/O):** And McCrory takes a left hook to the head...he's down again.

*Glenn falls.*

**COMMENTATOR (V/O):** One.

*He tries to get back up but can't.*

**GLENN:** The second time down - I couldn't get up... the brain is telling you to stand but the co-ordination has gone...your legs disobey you...the strength has left your arms...you feel helpless. Visions of belts, titles and glory evaporate...the past seven years - all the hard work, the endless hours of running, sparring, skipping, sweating...the sacrifice...the pain *(tearful)* a complete waste of time.

*He falls flat on his back.*

**COMMENTATOR (V/O):** Two.

**GLENN:** I'm sorry David.

**COMMENTATOR (V/O):** Three.

**GLENN:** The dream's over.

**COMMENTATOR (V/O):** Four.

**GLENN:** (*a bit angry*) This is reality!

**COMMENTATOR (V/O):** Five.

**GLENN:** (*angrier*) Don't give me that crap!

**COMMENTATOR (V/O):** Six.

**GLENN:** (*angry*) How can you say I let you down?

**COMMENTATOR (V/O):** Seven.

**GLENN:** (*angry*) No, you sod off!

**COMMENTATOR (V/O):** Eight.

**GLENN:** (*less angry*) I said it second.

**COMMENTATOR (V/O):** Nine.

**GLENN:** (*beat*) Help me little brother.

**COMMENTATOR (V/O):** Ten.

*Bell/cheers/noise.*

**GLENN:** And McCrory's counted out...he doesn't know where he is or even what he's doing.

*Glenn stands, head bowed.*

**MAN (V/O):** What an inglorious swansong for the former contender.

*Noise fades.*

*Simon and Garfunkel's "The Boxer" as light fades.*

*Blackout.*

**S&G (V/O):** (*sings*)...I am leaving, I am leaving; but the fighter still remains, la, la, la, la, la.

## END OF ACT ONE

# ACT TWO

*Props: A stool, boxing gloves, bucket (containing a bit of water and sponge, bottled water and towel). To the right, a sports bag and overcoat.*

*Blackout.*

*Orange Juice's "Rip It Up" is the last song on the song list.*

**V/O:** (*sings*) When I first saw you
Something stirred within me
You were standing sultry in the rain
If I could've held you
I would've held you
Rip it up and start again

*Image "Round 7. Rip it up and start again".*

**V/O:** (*sings*) Rip it up and start again
Rip it up and start again
I hope to God you're not as dumb as you make out
I hope to God (*fades*)

**MALE (V/O):** Seconds out. Round 7. Rip it up and start again.

*Lights up.*

*Glenn sits on the edge of the stage with a scrapbook.*

**GLENN:** David's scrapbook...*(opens it)* a small press cutting from October 8, 1986

"Hughroy Currie beat Glenn McCrory in a heavyweight bout last night. The two-round knock-out was McCrory's fourth successive defeat."

I'd become a footnote!

This was the newspaper that only two and a half years ago was calling me the "White Bruno".

*He stands.*

**GLENN:** Mandy and I should never have got married - we were both too young, volatile and...in debt.

But hey, this was Thatcher's Britain - lots of my people were in the same boat - living on credit...two pay days from bankruptcy.

The steel industry was decimated, the mines were being closed down and shipbuilding on the Tyne and the Wear was being ravaged.

And I wanted sympathy!

To get out of the house, I often popped round to see David.

*Image : David.*

**GLENN:** Where's David's electric wheelchair, mam?

**MAM (V/O):** Don't mention that electric wheelchair to me! They took it off him - he was a danger to humanity!

**GLENN:** David was now attending a day centre. At home he was immobile.

Mam, being mam, soldiered on...a 24-hour carer - a real hero...she found solace in writing poetry...it was printed in the *Evening Chronicle* and she's had a book published - it's available online!

David, being David, never complained...he loved beating everyone at chess...and just smiled. He was always smiling...sometimes that pissed me right off!

(*to David's image, angry*) What have you got to smile about, eh? (*beat*) Life!?

Here he was, defying death every single day - and I'm moping about, giving a boxer's "tale of woe" to anyone who would listen!

You know, David made me realise I had a beautiful daughter...I had my health - I'd never been hurt or marked in the ring - in fact, there was still a (*touches face*) cutting, rugged, dashing, handsomeness about this peachy-skinned face.

(*to audience*) What? I'd only just turned 22, remember!

*Glenn looks at scrapbook.*

**GLENN:** David had my career detailed...from the ABA

championship described in *Stanley News* to articles, photographs and features in *The Times, The Guardian, The Sun...Mirror...London Evening Standard...Boxing News.*

Prefaced next to my name were glowing accolades - the likes of which I'd dreamt of as a kid:

"The White Bruno"..."Golden Gloves"..."Contender".

I was a contender.

Was.

But you don't lose your skills in a year!

I'd been good.

Your biggest enemy is self belief.

I'm still good!

*Puts scrapbook down.*

*Image: Beau Williford.*

**GLENN:** Beau Williford from (*American*) Lafayette, Louisiana (*normal*) had seen me sparring in London in 1984 with Dennis Andries, the British Light-Heavyweight Champion, who was now world champion - Beau trained and advised him.

**BEAU (V/O):** (*American*) Hey, what happened to that impressive young fighter I saw in London?

**GLENN:** I told him my diet no longer consisted of

sausage, bacon, black pudding and gold top milk - I was losing weight...I'd been too heavy to fight my type of fight.

**BEAU (V/O):** (*American*) I knew that back then. You ain't a heavyweight and should never have been put in with the likes of Pika, Eklund and Currie.

**GLENN:** He'd been following my career! He saw I'd wasted more than two years as a never-to-be heavyweight.

**BEAU (V/O):** (*American*) You're a cruiserweight, Glenn - that's where your future lies...come over and see me...perhaps we can do something good together.

**GLENN:** Why aye.

**BEAU (V/O):** (*American*) What you say?

**GLENN:** Fantastic! Beau even paid for me to fly out to Lafayette.

*He dances and claps across the stage to a snatch of the tune of "America" (West Side Story).*

**GLENN:** He lined up a fight and put me up...in a storeroom full of junk - I slept on a settee.

*Music grinds to a halt.*

**GLENN:** I trained in a real ghetto area - I was the only white face there - I sparred with some pretty useful heavyweights...all of them wanted to rip my f-ing head off.

*He steps forward.*

**GLENN:** (*American*) Louisville, Kentucky (*normal*) the birthplace of Muhammad Ali.

My natural weight now was around 13 stone 8 pounds - top of the scale for cruiserweight.

I won the first fight easy enough...I was back on the winning trail.

Progress.

Beau even gave me a nickname.

> *Image: "Gentleman Glenn McCrory" jacket.*

**GLENN:** Gentleman Glenn McCrory! (*laughs and points to himself*) Gentleman!

I flew back to England for a few weeks over Christmas.

> *He dances and claps back across stage, singing "America" (Da, Da, Da, Da, etc).*

**GLENN:** I'd missed Victoria's first birthday...and our house had been repossessed...we were living with Mandy's mam.

> *Glenn signing on.*

**GLENN:** (*shouts*) Seasons greetings Stanley dole office...(*normal*) Ho, bloody, ho!

(*to Mandy, angry*) If you want a reliable guy with a 9 to 5 job, look elsewhere!

> *Sound of door slamming.*

**GLENN:** (*to audience*) I know, I know! You won't be the first people to think me irresponsible. I couldn't blame Mandy...she wanted security. But I wanted to conquer the world...and Beau had given me the lifeline of a career resurrection.

He lined up another fight for me in Houston, Texas.

Life was exciting...in America!

(*American*) And in the red corner...Calvin Sherman.

Sherman was a well-built gentleman - or as Beau said (*American*)) "freaking huge".

His nickname was "The Killer Monster".

*Glenn slowly looks up.*

**GLENN:** But I weighed in at 14 stone 8lb - the lightest I'd been since my professional debut back in 84. I was now fitter and quicker.

First round (*punches*) bang...I knocked him spark out.

The other thing that was coming back was my confidence.

Belief was my motivation...belief in myself - if you don't believe in yourself, who else will? I flew back to Newcastle with Beau for a tough fight against Danny Lawford.

I was thrilled to be based back in the North East.

My support was growing again. People were hearing about me returning to winning ways...

*Image: Doug Bidwell.*

**GLENN:** ...and I wa-

**DOUG (V/O):** Allo Glenn, my boy.

**GLENN:** Doug Bidwell - remember him?

**DOUG (V/O):** I think there's mileage in this idea of you being a cruiserweight.

**GLENN:** Doug, meet Beau.

**DOUG (V/O):** You're still under contract to me... remember?

**GLENN:** So then, Doug lined me up against Barry Ellis - the guy I beat in my first fight - three years ago! Hardly career developing stuff. *(to Doug)* Where? *(beat)* The West End? Benwell?

**DOUG (V/O):** London!

**GLENN:** I won on points.

In the dressing room afterwards...

Doug, can I have my money please?

**DOUG (V/O):** Listen Glenn. You weren't supposed to be on the bill tonight.

**GLENN:** What?

**DOUG (V/O):** Yeah...we had to fit you in at the last

moment and had to pay for your opponent from your share of the money-

**GLENN:** Bla, bla, bla...he listed his expenses, meals, hotels - the upshot was...

**DOUG (V/O):** You owe me 150 pounds.

**GLENN:** You what? It was then that I finally faced up to the fact that the loveable rogue Doug Bidwell and his slavery contract had to go...but I couldn't afford a solicitor, never mind take him to court.

*Image: "Round 8: The County Durham Rocky!"*

**MALE (V/O):** Seconds out Round 8: The County Durham Rocky!

**GLENN:** Now, Frank Warren...

*Image: Frank Warren.*

**GLENN:** ...is a top, top promoter but he always seemed to be in the opposite corner. One of his charges was Andy Straughn. Andy, a month previously - in February 1987 - had lost his British Cruiserweight title so Frank had arranged for Andy to fight an official eliminator - giving him an immediate opportunity to regain his crown.

I can imagine the conversation.

**WARREN (V/O):** Right, Andy, we need a "name".

**GLENN:** *(points to himself)* Tick.

**WARREN (V/O):** But someone who's past his best.

**GLENN:** Tick.

**WARREN (V/O):** Someone who'll take the fight at short notice.

**GLENN:** Tick.

**WARREN (V/O):** Someone who'll put up a reasonable show.

**GLENN:** Tick.

**WARREN (V/O):** Someone you'll definitely beat.

**GLENN:** Double tick.

**WARREN (V/O):** Get McCrory!

**GLENN:** Like I said, from contender to stepping stone fodder in 18 months! But what happened next was something akin to the Rocky movie.

*Uplifting music plays.*

**GLENN:** Step one: find a well-fitted gym in which to train. In the books I'd read, champions trained in old gyms with posters of the greats on the walls. The smell of sweat and testosterone seeped from the walls. Hopefuls honed their skills under the gaze of battle-hardened boxing sages. The air...dense with memories of classical bouts fought in bygone eras.

*Music grinds to a halts.*

**GLENN:** *(beat)* My gym was nowt like that! When I say Rocky - I don't mean the Hollywood Rocky...I'm talking County Durham Rocky here!

A gym?! Ha, it was a small, derelict room above a fruit shop in Catchgate, near Annfield Plain.

Step two: find a sponsor to pay the rent.

Thank you...Stanley dole office.

Step three: Put up a punch bag.

To do this, we needed a large metal bar to fit across the room.

This entailed my brother Neil and me, um, scavenging... we'll say no more.

Step four: a shower and a toilet.

A shower...not essential.

A toilet?

A bucket in the corner would suffice.

Step five: a ring - no canvas and ordinary ropes.

*(to self)* Remember, Glenn... don't lean back on the ropes otherwise you'd hit the wall and plaster'll land on your head.

This was my gym...when I say gym, I mean a stinking craphole.

Step six: a top trainer.

*Image: Alan Walker and Glenn.*

**GLENN:** I pulled in Alan Walker, who I knew from my amateur days. His pro-game experience? Zilch!

But that wasn't the point, I already knew how to fight.

*Running on the spot.*

**GLENN:** Alan, every day, came running with me on the Consett moors...encouraging me.

**ALAN (V/O):** Run you lazy git!

**GLENN:** (*bent over*) Alan, man, I'm knackered.

**ALAN (V/O):** (*shouts*) Move it!

**GLENN:** Step seven: an experienced corner team.

My brother Neil and Uncle Anthony came on board.

Their boxing experience? None what-so-ever!

So here we were, a motley crew...and one punch bag!

*He shadow boxes punchball.*

**GLENN:** But I came into the fight weighing 13 stone 6 pounds - my lowest-ever fighting weight.

*Bell rings.*

**GLENN:** I won on a tenth round stoppage.

*He raises his hands.*

**GLENN:** My career was back with a vengeance.

And so was...

*Image: Doug Bidwell.*

**DOUG (V/O):** Glennnnnnnnnnnnn, my old son, what do you know about Chisanda Mutti?

*Image: Chisanda Mutti.*

**GLENN:** Mutti was a tough Zambian...he'd failed in two world title attempts but he was the reigning Commonwealth Cruiserweight champion

**DOUG (V/O):** Get ready to meet him, he's coming to Gateshead.

**GLENN:** My first thought was, "Who'd come to Gateshead for a holiday?"

**DOUG (V/O):** Gateshead Leisure Centre to defend his crown against you, my son.

**GLENN:** A title shot in the North East of England! Given the way my expectations had been well and truly lowered over the past year, I honestly thought this could be the pinnacle of my boxing career.

*Spars.*

**GLENN:** My left jab was good. And my left hook to the body and head could do some damage. But this thing (*holds up right hand*) chicken shit.

I was sparring when owwwwwwwwwwww!

*He clutches his left hand.*

**GLENN:** I caught his elbow.

Ahhh, the pain!

Doug had to cut my glove off...my thumb was bent back at almost 180 degrees...completely dislocated. Newcastle General Hospital - they couldn't put my thumb back. Four hours later:

**DOCTOR (V/O):** I'm afraid we'll have to operate Mr McCrory.

**GLENN:** No way, doctor, please no.

The Mutti fight was only four weeks away, this is surely my last chance!

Please give it one last go, doctor.

*We hear a crack and the thumb is straight.*

**GLENN:** "Ouch! That hurt somewhat," I said politely, as the thumb popped back into place.

Did I bollocks (*screams and holds hand*).
Owwwwwwwwwwwwwwww (*slowly looks up at audience, embarrassed*) (*gently*) Ow!

I was put in a plaster cast.

**DOCTOR (V/O):** Mr McCrory, if you come back on September 15 we'll remove it.

**GLENN:** Thanks doct…What? The 15th? I'm fighting for the Commonwealth title on the 4th!

So here I am on the 4th.

Gateshead Leisure Centre.

The previous four weeks were spent shadow boxing and sparring with my right hand.

I cut the plaster off the day before.

The first time I used my left hand in a month was against Mutti…in the ring.

*Bell rings.*

**GLENN:** Round five. Déjà vu.

**DOUG (V/O):** Knock him out, knock him out!

**GLENN:** Knock him out! Mutti was a raging bull.

**DOUG (V/O):** Knock him out, knock him out!

**GLENN:** Knock him out, my backside. I stood in a neutral corner so I didn't have to listen to any more of Doug's crap.

**V/O:** And the new commonwealth champion is Glenn McCrory.

**GLENN:** A points decision...my first professional title. And still on the dole!

*Image: "Round 9. Mike Who?"*

**MALE (V/O):** Seconds out Round 9: Mike who?

**GLENN:** Three days later, Beau called from America...I couldn't believe my ears.

*Image: Mike Tyson.*

**GLENN:** At this time "Iron" Mike Tyson was the biggest name in world boxing. He wore black shorts, no socks and had no dressing gown.

*Puts towel over shoulders a la Tyson.*

**GLENN:** He walked into the ring with a towel over his head which he would throw off aggressively...

*He throws off towel a la Tyson then imitates him oozing menace.*

**GLENN:** ...and then prowl around, oozing menace.

He was the meanest of meanest mother...kissers!

Word from Tyson's training camp was that he was knocking out top heavyweights for fun...some of his sparring partners were doing moonlight flits rather than face him.

**BEAU (V/O):** Glenn? Are you still there, Glenn?

**GLENN:** *(scared)* Yes.

And so, I agreed to spar with Tyson in preparation for his world title fight with Tyrell Biggs.

Tyson had just signed a seven-fight deal with HBO worth...26.5 million dollars.

My wage was two...wait for it...two hundred dollars...around £200 by today's money, probably less...for six days a week.

Before flying out, I called at mam's house. Dad slipped me £20. Thanks, Dad. Mam said David's got something to give you.

*Glenn squats to pick up the rosary from David.*

**GLENN:** With a mighty effort, David gave me his rosary beads...they'd been with him since he was a child - his only possession in the orphanage, and truth be told, his only worldly possession now.

*(jokingly)* I am coming back, David!

*(to audience)* I hoped!

Tyson's camp had paid for an economy return plane ticket - which I figured I would use quickly enough. A final check of my hand luggage...headguard, gloves, gumshield...clean underwear. My suitcase contained the rest of my gear.

**AIRPORT VOICE (V/O):** *(American)* Welcome to Philadelphia, Pennsylvania...have a nice day.

**GLENN:** Have a nice day! In the stretch limo, I was surrounded by Tyson's people - six of the biggest blokes I'd ever seen. One said: *(American)* Welcome to casualty central!

The others laughed (*Glenn imitiates laughter*).

The limo driver said: (*American*) Where would you like to be?

I said "with my suitcase" - it was mislaid somewhere in Australia!

Seriously!

Next day I used the money dad had given me to buy new gear. I had to face the meanest man on the planet having not slept the night before and wearing:

A pair of cheap white shorts.

A white T-shirt.

And a pair of plimsolls.

Tyson looked me up and down, held out his glove...

*Touches glove.*

**GLENN:** ...and smiled.

(*as Tyson*) Great to meet you, Glenn. Thank you very much for coming.

What a nice, well-mannered, young chap, I thought. Once we were in the ring...

(*as Tyson*) I'm gonna kill you, you motherf***er. I'm gonna rip your white honky head off.

(*to audience*) Eeeeeeh, I thought, Ali would never have said that. And then I thought, he's never been up against a Stanley lad...one with nothing to lose!

*Glenn spars.*

**GLENN:** For four rounds I'd whacked him with jabs. I looked at Tyson and said: "You're not so hot, Mike baby!" (*stops, to audience*) I never actually said it out loud, y'knaa.

That was it – I was part of the camp...respect! I looked around at the sparring team:

*Image: All three on screen together - James Broad, Oliver McCall and James Tillis.*

James Broad, Oliver McCall, James Tillis

Some of the top heavyweights in the world.

I'd just turned 23, and the only white face there.

*Image: "Tyson v Biggs. October 1987".*

**GLENN:** Seventh round, Tyson unleashed an uppercut that floored Biggs and almost sent him out of the ring. With that momentous punch, Iron Mike unified the three world heavyweight boxing titles: WBC, WBA and IBF...he was only 21 years old.

*Image: Glenn and Mike Tyson.*

**GLENN:** Afterwards, the man on his way to becoming arguably the greatest-ever fighting machine, hugged me. (*as Tyson*) You did that, Glenn...stick around, man.

The invite was to be Mike's chief sparring partner for what would be his 4th round destruction of Larry Holmes. I'd get 1,500 dollars a week. I'd never earned that amount for a fight, and I was Commonwealth champion, remember. I had another reason to remain involved in the camp.

*Image: Tee Jay.*

**GLENN:** I was lined up for the British cruiserweight title, against Tee Jay. I couldn't afford sparring partners, so what could be better preparation for a fight?

In total, I sparred 96 rounds with Mike Tyson - when Tyson was in his absolute prime - that's 288 minutes...nearly five hours. He never put me down once - and I even blacked his eye. He still reminds me about that.

London, January 21, 1988...almost four years since my first pro fight. Tee Jay was a good opponent. But I won it pretty comprehensively in 12 rounds.

I was now British and Commonwealth Champion.

A week later, I thought I'd scored another victory...the British Boxing Board of Control decreed...

**BBBC MAN (V/O):** Mr McCrory, you are now out of the contract with Doug Bidwell...

**GLENN:** Brilliant! Thank you.

**BBBC MAN (V/O):** ...but you must pay him 25 per cent of your boxing earnings until the end of the contract term.

**GLENN:** Another two years! And I thought these people

were supposed to be on my side?

I got £2,000 for winning the British title - out of that I had to give a quarter to Doug Bidwell, 33 per cent to Beau and pay my team.

It was back to Stanley dole office on the Monday.

*Image: "Round 10: The wrong guy"*

**MALE (V/O):** Seconds out. Round 10: The wrong guy

*Image: Cedric Kushner.*

**GLENN:** In the Tyson camp, I'd caught the eye of Cedric Kushner - a major American promoter. Evander Holyfield had relinquished the undisputed cruiserweight titles in order to move up to heavyweight. He was WBC, WBA and IBF champion - that meant three world title belts were up for grabs...and six fighters would get an opportunity to fight for them.

John Gibson from the *Evening Chronicle* wrote:

"There are some decent cruiserweights...but there is only one person that everyone fears."

It wasn't me!

*Image: Patrick Lumumba.*

**GLENN:** It was this guy.

A Swedish-based Kenyan called Patrick Lumumba. Nobody wanted to fight him for two reasons:

Firstly: Being a Kenyan and living in Sweden, he had no fan base...this meant the purse would be poor.

Secondly: He was mean!

As World Amateur Champion, out of over 300 bouts Lumumba had lost only six! Incredible! Among Lumumba's professional conquests were former world cruiserweight champion Alfonzo Ratliff and future champion Jeff Lampkin.

In August '87 he'd lost a controversial 10-round decision to James Broad, the former North American Boxing Federation Heavyweight Champion. In the first round he knocked Broad almost comatose...Lumumba was giving away...five stones four pounds.

Managed by Don King, Lumumba was now sparring in New York with Mike Tyson - and word was he was knocking Mike around. Lumumba was definitely the man to avoid.

The others...no worries.

And then I got the call from Cedric.

*Image: Cedric Kushner.*

**CEDRIC (V/O):** (*American*) Glenn, we've got you an IBF world title fight.

**GLENN:** Yes!

**CEDRIC (V/O):** (*American*) You can have it in the North

East of Inger-land.

**GLENN:** Yes!

My mind raced. Who would it be? Carlos De Leon... a former champion...I could punch holes in him!

Belbouli, a French-Tunisian...bring him on!

**CEDRIC (V/O):** (*American*) Patrick Lumumba.

**GLENN:** Bollocks!

Patrick Lumumba was nicknamed "Killer".

He'd only had ten professional fights in five years because no one wanted to fight him - including me!

The good news was the world title fight meant Mandy and me had been able to secure a mortgage on a small terraced house in Station Road, Stanley.

Little did the bank know my fee for the Lumumba fight was only $15,000. Out of that I had to pay my team...as well as Doug Bidwell his 25 per cent and Beau Williford 33 per cent.

My cut?

£4,000 by today's money.

Go figure!

*He has scrapbook.*

**GLENN:** When I left home, David took my boxing posters off the bedroom wall and placed them in here for safekeeping.

(*turns pages*) Boxing champions from *The Ring* magazine.

Perhaps...perhaps...I'd soon be in the centre pages...the first world champion from the North East of England.

(*puts scrapbook in sporting bag*) Now, I'm not a betting man, but I'd put money on the fact that I was the only fighter in modern history who signed on just two days before fighting for a world title!

(*shouts*) Thank you Stanley dole office!

*Image: (The Sun back page) - "Glenn's a goner".*

**MALE (V/O):** Seconds out Round 11: Glenn's a Goner.

**GLENN:** Saturday, June 3, 1989.

David had been written off by doctors years ago - he wasn't expected to live much beyond 15. He was now 23...and determined to see me as world champion.

Watching your brother slowly die...not being able to do anything for himself. (*he reflects*) I put this fight into context...occasionally I fought tough men...every day David fought death. His spirit was ferocious. And these...people...had the audacity to write me off! Before the fight, we listened to *Wind Beneath My Wings*...David's favourite song.

(*sings Wind Beneath My Wings*) Did you ever know that you're my hero and everything I would like to be?

*Images: "Round 12: Death or Glory".*

**MALE (V/O):** Seconds out Round 12: Death or glory.

*Putting on overcoat and picking up sports bag and making his way off stage.*

**GLENN:** I kissed Victoria, and then Mandy...on the cheek. She had a seat in the auditorium...somewhere. I walked the 200 yards from our house to the Louisa Centre...bag over my shoulder, like usual. I could see people milling around, some in dinner jackets and a couple of limos passed by. There were television vans and film crews. I wondered what was happening in Stanley tonight...seriously.

Then, on the steps of Louisa Centre, it dawned. People were looking at me, pointing, some applauded. Patting me on the shoulders...asking for autographs.

**MALE FAN 1 (V/O):** Good luck, Glenn.

**GLENN:** Cheers.

**MALE FAN 2 (V/O):** Proud of you, Glenn.

**GLENN:** Thanks.

One bloke said *(tearful)* "This'll be the greatest day of my life, Glenn...if you win." Bloody hell, no pressure then!

*He exits stage, into auditorium.*

**GLENN:** For one night only, the former mining town of

Stanley in County Durham had become the centre of world boxing. The venue officially held 1,500 but 2,000 people rammed the hall.

*He stops to take off his coat.*

**GLENN:** Pre-fight, the only people in the changing room with me were my priest and my mate John Gibson, the *Evening Chronicle* journalist. A priest and a journalist? Aren't these the people who accompany condemned prisoners on Death Row?

*Glenn exits via side door/back of the hall to get changed for his big entrance.*

*A cocophony of lights flashing and music (ITV Sports music theme).*

*We're now at the fight. Three ropes projected on screen, lights flash.*

**COMPERE (V/O):** Ladies and gentlemen, welcome to the main event of the evening, the International Boxing Federation cruiserweight world title.

In the blue corner from Kenya, boxing out of New York, wearing black shorts and weighing in at 13 stone 5 pounds, put your hands together for Patrick Lumumba.

*Brief film footage of Lumumba waving at audience.*

*Sound "Fanfare For The Common Man."*

*Glenn appears at entrance. He's wearing red shorts, white hand bandages and boxing boots (ready for action with towel on his shoulders).*

**COMPERE (V/O):** And from Annfield Plain, Derwentside, wearing red shorts and weighing in at 13 stone 8 pounds...Glenn McCrory

*Loud cheers and encouragement as Glenn enters stage via "the ropes" and holds his arms aloft as he parades in the ring.*

*He limbers up then puts his gloves on as he speaks.*

**GLENN:** I looked over at Lumumba's corner...the five-to-one-on favourite casually waved at the crowd like he'd just turned up to collect the title...my title!

Beau was subdued, the people in my corner were saying nothing.

But the noise kept growing.

People were clapping, cheering, sticking their thumbs up.

**MALE FAN 1 (V/O):** Howay Glenn!

**GLENN:** If I was a gonner, the people of Stanley certainly hadn't read the script...the noise became thunderous.

**MALE FAN 2 (V/O):** You can do it, Glenn!

**FEMALE FAN (V/O):** Howay Glenn!

**GLENN:** (*bangs gloves together*) This is it, bonny lad. It's what you've worked 10 years for.

12 rounds...36 minutes from the dream.

One chance...one crack only.

**CHANTS (V/O):** McCrory, McCrory, McCrory.

**GLENN:** Listen to them...just listen!

**CHANTS (V/O):** McCrory, McCrory, McCrory!

**GLENN:** Breathe it in.

**MALE FAN 1 (V/O):** Go on Glenn!

**FEMALE FAN (V/O):** Howay Glenn!

**GLENN:** This small ring is now your entire world...your zone. You no longer hear the crowd...your peripheral vision is just a blur as you focus on the man not four feet away...the man who wants to inflict pain.

The concentration is intense.

One slip and you're hurt...finished.

I, Glenn George McCrory, am prepared to die tonight...are you Patrick Lumumba?

**ANNOUNCER (V/O):** Seconds out, round one.

*Bell rings. Cheers. Glenn boxes.*

**GLENN:** The bell brings an adrenaline surge...fear and doubts evaporate. Constantly processing his movement...backwards, forwards, the way he sways...his body language...watching his eyes...dodging the jab...constantly vigilant for that destructive left hook.

I jab.

It's flowing nicely.

A couple connect.

It feels good...it's important to dent his confidence early on.

Another jab hits home...and another.

Two and a half minutes in.

I've got him on the back foot and shuffling into his corner.

I follow up with some sharp shots.

To the body.

To the head.

*Crowd cheers.*

**GLENN:** He's off guard. Left jab, left jab...probing for the opening...a mili-second is all I need.

*Glenn throws left hook.*

*Sound: Boom.*

*Lighting denotes punch.*

**COMMENTATOR (V/O):** And McCrory has launched a mighty left hook.

*Crowd cheers.*

**GLENN:** His legs buckle...he's almost down. His eyes, a few seconds ago so confident and arrogant, are now bloodshot and rolling in his head.

He's in no-man's land, struggling to stand up...leaning on the ropes. I launch myself at him...unleashing a flurry of punches.

Bang, bang, bang.

*Sound: Boom.*

*Lighting denotes punch.*

**GLENN:** I catch him on the chin...his head goes back but he stays on his feet.

He grabs me.

I push him off...jabbing, jabbing...looking for any weakness but he covers up, taking good shots to his arm, stomach and chest.

His whole body's limp as he clings on to me.

The crowd are baying for him to fall.

**COMMENTATOR (V/O):** The bell can't come soon enough for the Kenyan.

**GLENN:** I'm lining up the knockout punch.

*We hear the bell.*

**GLENN:** (*angry*) Bollocks!

*Glenn watches Lumumba back to his corner.*

**GLENN:** He's unsteady on his feet.

**ANNOUNCER (V/O):** Seconds out round two.

*Sound: Bell.*

**GLENN:** His cockiness has gone but the eyes are focused. I go for him right from the off...finish it, Glenn, come on, son!

I catch him again with a raking left.

*Sound: Boom.*

*Lighting denotes punch.*

*Crowd roars.*

**GLENN:** But it doesn't have the same effect as the first big punch. He presses on and lands a couple of incisive stomach blows. His eyes are back to normal and he's focusing...staring hard...weighing me up.

I jab...he ducks...he's quick.

He throws a rally - the punches miss but he's just getting his range.

I jab...catching him again and again...but he strikes back.

*Sound: Boom.*

*Lighting denotes punch and Glenn is stunned.*

**COMMENTATOR (V/O):** A good left from the Kenyan.

**GLENN:** He stuns me. The crowd goes silent. It's a surreal moment.

For a split second everything moves in slow motion and then normality returns. For some reason I smell the stench of stale tobacco. I see him bearing down on me, malice in his eyes.

I bob left to miss his jab.

He jabs again, I duck...and launch my own double jab...they land.

*Crowd cheers.*

**GLENN:** Another sweet left hook.

*Sound: Boom.*

*Lighting denotes punch.*

**COMMENTATOR:** Lumumba is on the ropes...he's clinging on frantically.

**GLENN:** I rain in with body punches. Each time I connect there's an involuntary gasp from him.

Go down...go down, man.

But he won't fall.

He's hanging on...punch after punch after punch.

I push him away but he's holding on to the ropes.

Go down, man!

Crack!

*Sound: Boom.*

*Lighting denotes punch.*

**GLENN:** A clean left to his jaw, sends his gumshield flying.

*Crowd cheers.*

**GLENN:** Go down, man...please just drop. I land another corking left hook.

*Sound: Boom.*

*Lighting denotes punch.*

**GLENN:** This time, surely.

*Bell rings.*

**GLENN:** (*looks at Lumumba*) Twice in two rounds he's been saved by the bell.

*Glenn sits.*

*The crowd cheers.*

**ANNOUNCER (V/O):** Seconds out round three.

*Bell rings.*

*Glenn gets up to fight.*

**GLENN:** I can't believe it...he's off his stool quickly and looks around the crowd...just to let them know he's still in the game. He throws a few body punches that connect and a couple of jabs that sting. We're toe to toe in the centre of the ring and he lands with a right cross to my head and then a cutting right to my ribs...it hurts. He's getting stronger and catches me a couple of times...he's winning the round.

I hear Beau shouting.

**BEAU (V/O):** Jab...jab...move, box!

**GLENN:** Lumumba's right eye is swelling but he keeps pressing forward...catching me with some good jabs...they rattle me.

Come on Glenn, concentrate!

It's a hard round this... I manage a couple of jabs...then a left-right combination...an opening...I connect with a peach of a left hook.

*Sound: Boom.*

*Lighting denotes punch.*

**GLENN:** The crowd cheers even before his legs buckle.

**COMMENTATOR (V/O):** Lumumba is in trouble again.

**GLENN:** Despite my big finish, he'd won the third round.

*Glenn goes to his corner.*

**ANNOUNCER (V/O):** Seconds out round four,

*Bell rings.*

*Glenn takes a few punches.*

**GLENN:** He's really coming into the fight now. I'm looking to unleash the ultimate left hook...but I can't afford to be outscored waiting to land it...everything is about vigilance.

Another one-two combination leaves him unsteady.

I look for another big finish to the round...he's leaning on me.

Constantly pushing away a 14-and-a-half stone man saps your strength.

*Bell rings and Glenn sits on stool.*

**GLENN:** Beau tells me that Lumumba's work rate is dropping after each round.

He pulls my face to his.

**BEAU (V/O):** Are you listening?

**GLENN:** Yes...of course.

*Bell rings and Glenn gets up to fight.*

**ANNOUNCER (V/O):** Seconds out round five.

**GLENN:** We swap some decent punches...it's pulsating...incessant.

Lumumba scores with a couple of jabs.

He's now working inside.

Watch his head, watch his head.

I take four punches without reply and fall back onto the ropes...I desperately need a breather.

He senses this and lands a left hook to my head.

*Sound: Boom.*

*Lighting denotes punch.*

**GLENN:** It hurts...he moves in to land another blow but I move aside and connect with a perfect straight right.

*Sound: Boom.*

*Lighting denotes punch.*

**COMMENTATOR (V/O):** Oh, McCrory, right at the death of the round, has Lumumba in trouble again.

**GLENN:** He takes five more rapid punches.

**COMMENTATOR:** The crowd are on their feet at the back of hall.

*Crowd Cheers. Bell sounds.*

**GLENN:** (*watches Lumumba*) He staggers back to the corner but my energy levels are dropping too.

*Glenn sits.*

**GLENN:** Beau is animated...he's shadow boxing...jabbing.

*Bell sounds and Glenn gets up to fight.*

**GLENN:** The start of another round...which one? I've lost count. He comes to meet me in the centre of the ring.

I jab...and catch him with a right.

But he keeps coming forward and then starts doing things I'd never seen or experienced before.

He steps to the right and throws two right hands to the side of my head - one skids off the top, the other lands on my ear.

*We hear a loud piercing noise.*

**GLENN:** What the hell?

He moves in again and hits me in the same place.

*Loud piercing noise.*

**GLENN:** And again.

*Loud piercing noise.*

**GLENN:** He's perforated my eardrum! The bastard!

Our heads clash.

The referee parts us.

I catch him with a clean body punch...air gushes from his lungs.

I push him back...he stays on the ropes, gasping for breath. My punches rain in...I'm looking for an opening but he's ducking and weaving...all the time recovering. A few of his stray, defensive punches land on my right ear and the ear-piercing noise cuts into me.

*High pitched sound.*

**GLENN:** I counter with a sweet right hook square on the chin.

*Sound: Boom.*

*Lighting denotes punch.*

*Crowd Cheers.*

**GLENN:** I've knocked strong men spark out with a shot like that but this guy's still standing. I'm feeling drained of energy now and his resilience drains me even more.

He lands a jab to my jaw...it momentarily stuns me.

I'm not marked...all the pain is within...but my mouth is cut inside. Any sight of blood and he'd be in for the kill. Don't spit it out...swallow. It leaves a sour taste in the back of my throat.

I deliver three more precise jabs.

He's taken everything I've got...and he's still coming forward, like a panther stalking its prey.

This is when the doubts start. Perhaps my chance went in the first round.

Come on Glenn, concentrate. He advances...I take body punches and another piercing left hook to the head.

*We hear a loud piercing noise.*

**GLENN:** Everything slows down...life flashes by in slow motion for a split second and then back to usual speed.

Everything becomes clear...I pick out individual voices in the crowd.

I hear dad shouting "Jab, Glenn"...pleading..."box, son".

My enemy's out of focus...where is he?

I'm vulnerable.

I have to get back into the zone quickly.

Back up...jab...that's good.

Concentrate...he's all that matters.

Keep moving.

A double jab...left...right...constantly probing.

And then it comes...in the blink of an eye.

*Glenn delivers a left hook.*

*Sound: Boom.*

*Lighting denotes punch.*

**COMMENTATOR (V/O):** Oh, McCrory has delivered a

left hook bang on the chin. Lumumba's legs buckle again.

*Bell rings.*

**GLENN:** Bollocks!

By the seventh round his guard is beginning to drop.

How much do you want it Glenn? How much?

**CHANTS (V/O):** McCrory, McCrory, McCrory.

**ANNOUNCER (V/O):** Seconds out, round 8.

*Bell rings.*

**GLENN:** He's still staying with me.

My game plan...stay out of range, bide my time...pace it nicely.

**COMMENTATOR (V/O):** I think McCrory knows he's got this in the bag if he doesn't do anything stupid.

**GLENN:** I manage to slip his punches. The pace is dropping off.

But then I catch him with a left hook to the head and he's falling back onto the ropes...clinging on.

His rate of recovery has fallen considerably.

He's covering up.

My jabs pump but they're getting weaker...my arms feel like lead.

*Bell rings.*

*Glenn sits.*

**COMMENTATOR:** This will come down to stamina, guts, willpower and desire. Who wants it the most?

**ANNOUNCER (V/O):** Seconds out, round 9.

*Bell rings and Glenn gets up to fight.*

**GLENN:** He keeps landing menacing punches...a straight right crashes into my head

*Sound: Boom.*

*Lighting denotes punch.*

**GLENN:** I counter with another raking left hook and a right catches him on the temple. The more he keeps coming, the more I hit him...punches to the body...another left hook to his chin.

*Sound: Boom.*

*Lighting denotes punch.*

*Crowd cheers.*

**COMMENTATOR (V/O):** Britain could have a new world champion here...but there are still three rounds to go.

**ANNOUNCER (V/O):** Seconds out, Round 10.

*Bell rings.*

**GLENN:** By my reckoning I'd landed six blistering left hooks on his head. I knew they've taken a lot out of him but he's still dangerous. Just to prove it, he catches me with a right uppercut. I see the punch coming but I'm so tired I can't get away.

*Sound: Boom.*

*Lighting denotes punch.*

**GLENN:** I return with a left hook...it uses vital energy but it connects and puts him on the ropes.

His gloves go down.

This could be my moment.

He takes five more punches with nothing in return.

I'm ahead by miles but I can't keep this pace up.

It's frenetic...relentless.

I'd tried everything...every move, every trick I know and he's still coming at me.

This is where the training kicks in...the hundreds of road miles, the endless sparring...the pain.

*Bell rings.*

**GLENN:** Thank God!

*Glenn sits and takes off his boxing gloves, drinks water, sponges his face with a towel as he speaks.*

**COMMENTATOR (V/O):** McCrory knows how to face this...as long as he doesn't do anything silly...or Lumumba finds one big bomb.

**GLENN:** Six minutes from victory. But I'm sapped. Six minutes is a long time in the ring, an eternity when there's nothing left in the tank. This is a guy who stopped his last five opponents and is still capable of landing one good punch. The thought of getting this close and losing is unbearable.

How could I let these people down? But my limbs feel like dead weights...major doubts flood my brain.

Beau is talking...I see his mouth move and I can hear him but I just can't take in what he's saying.

My eyes drift to the crowd...it's just a blur of colours and animated faces.

That's when it happened!

To a person the Stanley crowd started stomping and chanting my name.

*We hear stomping and chants of "McCrory, McCrory, McCrory."*

*Glenn is off his seat looking out.*

**CHANT (V/O):** McCrory, McCrory, McCrory.

**GLENN:** It was hypnotic...it felt like everyone in the auditorium was chanting and stomping. I looked over and saw David and mam...even mam was stomping. I knew then I would be leaving this ring either on a stretcher or holding a world champion's belt...possibly both! I knew I had to take him where he didn't want to go. I had to take him into the trenches...I had to take him down to hell.

**ANNOUNCER (V/O):** Seconds out, round 11.

*Bell rings and Glenn starts to spar.*

**GLENN:** I knew he had to come at me. He threw a couple of decent punches early on but then I hit him on the side of the head.

He's hanging on the ropes again and he's not bouncing back like he did.

He's facing defeat and he knows it.

Come on Glenn, come on.

**COMMENTATOR (V/O):** Lumumba looks desperately, desperately tired...a minute to go in round 11...the crowd are off their seats...stomping.

**GLENN:** I pummel him with body punches.

I'm possessed.

(*punches*) To the head, to the body.

Welcome to hell, Patrick.

**COMMENTATOR (V/O):** Lumumba can find nothing.

**GLENN:** Go down...go down.

*Bell rings.*

*Crowd cheers*

**COMMENTATOR (V/O):** McCrory is only three minutes away from becoming champion of the world.

*Glenn stays standing.*

**GLENN:** I can't sit down...not now.

*The stomping's getting louder.*

**GLENN:** That sense of destiny is within my grasp.

**CHANTS (V/O):** McCrory, McCrory, McCrory.

**GLENN:** Sing you beauties, sing!

Come on, come on...ring the bell, man...ring the bell.

Beau shouts.

**BEAU (V/O):** Stay out of trouble and it's yours.

**ANNOUNCER (V/O):** Seconds out, the 12th and final round.

*Bell rings.*

*Cheers.*

**GLENN:** Round 12...three minutes...180 seconds...what have you got left Patrick? He comes out at me...I duck, dive...his best shots are missing by miles.

I hit him with another left hook.

*Sound: Boom.*

*Lighting denotes punch.*

*Crowd cheers.*

**CHANTS (V/O):** McCrory, McCrory, McCrory.

**GLENN:** He reels back onto the ropes.

Don't follow up...120 seconds to go...stand your ground let him come at you.

He approaches again.

This time I deflect the punch and we're in a clinch.

I catch the smell of his perspiration.

A shower of sweat from his brow goes into my eyes.

I'm temporary blinded...step back, step back.

He comes at me again but I dodge the right hook...we clinch.

He's breathing heavily.

What's he got left?

60 seconds.

I shuffle and attack, landing a couple of jabs and a body punch, he moves back.

45 seconds...stay back, Glenn, stay back...let him come to you.

40 seconds...another left to his head...he falls back and leans on the ropes.

His eyes...blood red...are those of a beaten man.

Another clinch...the referee breaks us up.

I pull back quickly in case he tries a sneaky right hook, he does but it misses.

20 seconds...Beau's shouting "back off, stay back".

I take a few steps back - he follows me.

10 seconds.

He throws his last punch...I deflect it...I grab him and we lean on the ropes.

Five seconds.

I'm pummelling away in beat with the stomping.

Boom, boom, boom, boom.

*Bell rings.*

*Glenn falls to his knees.*

*Crowd cheers.*

**COMMENTATOR (V/O):** And surely, surely...Glenn McCrory, unless the judges have just arrived from Mars, is champion of the world.

*The crowd goes silent.*

**GLENN:** An eerie silence descends. The world stands still...the MC pauses to increase the tension.

**COMPERE (V/O):** By a unanimous decision, the undisputed...

**GLENN:** Then come the words I'd dreamt of hearing since a skinny 12-year-old walked into Consett Amateur Boxing Club.

**COMPERE (V/O):** ...and new Cruiserweight Champion of the World...Glenn McCrory.

*Cheers.*

**GLENN:** The noise was deafening.

*On screen: Glenn being held aloft.*

**GLENN:** I was lifted shoulder high and paraded around the ring. Everywhere I looked people were cheering...total strangers cuddled...it felt like the whole of Stanley was in tears.

And then, I saw the person who had made it all possible.

David had made it to see me proclaimed champion of the world.

It was the happiest moment of my life.

Two brothers - one fight.

The MC then hands me the microphone.

Silence descends.

This was my great *Rocky* moment.

I thought about quoting Oscar Wilde, Mohammad Ali...Dylan Thomas, Keats, Shelley...I was searching for glorious words, inspirational words that'll be quoted alongside Churchill in history books, words so profound people will be recalling them for centuries to come.

Who do I thank?

Mam, dad, David, Mandy, Father Phelan, who died a year earlier and had never missed a fight, Beau and Alan Walker, everyone in my corner, my brothers and sisters, the people of Stanley, the people of the North East?

There were just too many.

I touched my cheek (*touches cheek*)...remembering the first time I'd carried David and he'd kissed me.

Then the words came: Stanley dole office...I'm not coming back!

*Black out.*

*Image: (side by side) David with "David McCrory. 1966-1996" and Glenn with the world title belt.*

*Glenn turns to the images and clenches fist.*

*We hear "The Wind Beneath My Wings"*

**SINGER:** (*sings*) Did you ever know that you're my hero ....and everything I would like to be? I can fly higher than an eagle, cos you're the wind beneath my wings (*fades*).

*Lights up.*

*Glenn bows to audience.*

## THE END

# About Ed Waugh

Ed became a full-time creative writer in 2002. He was born on January 18, 1959. A home birth at 4 Tarset Place, Grange Estate, Gosforth, Newcastle (then Northumberland), Ed reckons this was because his lovely mam Elizabeth couldn't be prised away from watching Peyton Place.

In 1993, after attending Darlington Journalist College (where he met his marra and long-term collaborator Trevor Wood), Ed became a freelance journalist. Even earlier, after graduating from Sunderland Polytechnic in 1980, Ed was a political researcher during Thatcher's misrule. His writing proudly reflects his life-long campaigning work to transform society from one that exists for the benefit of the unaccountable wealthy - and privileged - few into a truly democratic one run by, and on behalf of, the many.

With Trevor Wood, Ed has co-written 14 plays, film scripts and a BBC radio sitcom. His solo plays are Dracula: Die Laughing (North East tour 2013 and Whitby Goth Festival, April 2014), The Accidental Activist (North East tour 2015, additional stand-up material by John Scott and John Gibson) and Mr Corvan's Music Hall (North East tour 2017). His new play Howay The Lasses, about female Munitionette footballers during WW1, will premiere at Gala Theatre, Durham in October 2021. In March/April 2022 he will premiere Wor Bella, a play about WW1 Blyth Spartans Ladies FC heroine Bella Reay.

He's written ten Laffalang shows directed by Gareth Hunter and featuring the Laffalang Gang at Stand, Newcastle, and Westovian Theatre, South Shields, and penned sketches for the annual Christmas at the Cathedral show in Newcastle and sketches for Sunday for Sammy with Trevor (2012 and 2014) and as a solo writer (2016, 2018 and 2020). His two radio sitcom pilots Where Did I Go Wrong? and Stand Up For Middle Age - were performed at The Word in South Shields in May 2018.

# Acknowledgements

It's been a privilege to see these three plays professionally performed in the region's top theatres. To have them preserved for posterity in a printed volume is an incredible thrill and honour; a wonderful bonus for our fantastic team. I'd particularly like to thank Arts Council England. Without Derek Tree (editor) you'd not be reading this.

My sincere apologies if I've left you out (alas, lack of space).

David Clasper, Dave Harker and Glenn McCrory: writers and friends, for the research in their brilliant books. Russell Floyd. Actors Jamie Brown, Micky Cochrane, Sarah Boulter and Wayne Miller. Musical arranger Jordan Miller. David Gibson.

**Hadaway Harry:** Richard Flood, Sophie Teasdale, Alison McGowan (puppet maker), Harriet Ghost, Micky McGregor, Craig Richardson. Gareth Hunter. Richard Barber, Tania Robinson. Philip Bernays, Nathan Reynard, Stuart Middleton and the Newcastle Theatre Royal marketing team.

**The Great Joe Wilson:** Pete Scott for his magnificent tunes to Joe's words (CDs available from JG Windows). Likewise Alex Glasgow. Johnny Handle, Brian and Helen Mawson, Ray Laidlaw, Phil Corbitt. From Darlington Hippodrome: Linda Winstanley, Alexander Edwards and Stephen Norman. Joe Wilson's Canadian family, especially Kasandra (Joe's great granddaughter).

**Carrying David:** Jane Harker, Les Robson. David Hull Promotions (Northern Ireland): David Hull, Conor Maguire and Russell Allardice. Tony Corcoran (Tyneside Irish Centre). Non-theatrical friends and family: Jane (this is all your fault!),

Ewan, Keir, Rachelle, Les R, Sylvia, Big Al, Linda, Tony, Eve, dad (Les), my late mam Elizabeth, Les and Viv.

And those who haven't missed a show: Chris, Lynn, David, Gayle, Michelle, Jen, Keith, Margaret, Brian, Joan, Hildred, Helen, Trevor, Pam. I'm not making these names up. There are dozens, hundreds more. Apologies for lack of space.

Ian Payne (Tyne Tees Television) for telling me about a forgotten Geordie rower called Harry Clasper, starting this exhilarating and erudite adventure rolling (and rolling).

To everyone who has been so supportive and enthusiastic, massive thanks.

### Dedicated to

### Willow and Everly
### Gan canny and fettle reetly wor bonny bairns.

*Ed Waugh photographed by Sophie Teasdale*

Ed Waugh